METAL THREAD EMBROIDERY

Tools, Materials and Techniques

METAL THREAD EMBROIDERY

Tools, Materials and Techniques

JANE LEMON

*And he made
the ephod of gold, blue and purple,
and scarlet, and fine twined linen.*

*And they did beat
the gold into thin plates, and cut it into wires,
to work it in the blue, and in the purple,
and in the scarlet, and in the fine
linen, with cunning work.*

(Exodus, 39: 2–3)

B. T. Batsford Ltd, London

To the memory of
MOLLIE COLLINS

A great exponent and lover of the technique

ISBN 0 7134 5577 2

Typeset by Latimer Trend & Company Ltd, Plymouth
and printed in Great Britain by R. J. Acford, Chichester, Sussex

for the publishers
B. T. Batsford Ltd.
4 Fitzhardinge Street
London W1H 0AH

Contents

Acknowledgements

Without the generous help and support of the Embroiderers' Guild and the Headquarters staff at Hampton Court, in allowing me use of the Collection and the Library, this book would never have been attempted. To Ann Sutton and Roma Mason go my gratititude for their generosity in allowing the use of their samplers and experimental pieces; to Margaret Nairn and Kathryn Salomon, my thanks for sharing their expertise.

I am also grateful to the following photographers for providing illustrations: Richard Goodchild; Tim Hutton; Harold Rose; Mark Singleton; Frank Taylor; and to Geoffrey Wheeler for making my own photographs look so good.

To all the people who gave access to the embroideries included in the book, and the embroiderers who provided examples of their work, my very grateful thanks.

To Leonie Mellish, who has typed, checked and sorted the book through long hours, my deep gratitude.

Finally, to Rachel Wright, my editor, go my sincere thanks.

Introduction

Metal thread work is the most exciting technique available to the embroiderer, and the skill needed to achieve all the possibilities with the best effect takes years of regular practice. It is the steady, practised rhythm of the expert that shows through in equally spaced couching stitches and an even tension on the laid threads. In the past, five or even seven years of full-time work was the usual term of apprenticeship, so we must accept that practice makes perfect!

Unfortunately, technique alone does not make an exquisite piece. It is essential to understand the materials that one is working with, since the movement of the threads in different directions and the placing of the varied textures all build up the play of light on this tonal work, accentuating the beauty of the metal.

Care should be taken, as in any embroidery, that too many methods are not included in one piece. This is perfectly acceptable, and in fact useful, for a sampler, but not for a finished article.

This book is written with the aim of helping the student of the technique, at any level. The alphabetical arrangement is intended to make the information easily available, with each kind of treatment gathered together for comparison and understanding. So that more experienced readers will not have to check through unwanted information, the book is divided into sections, '*Articles on which metal thread embroidery may be found*', '*Tools*', '*Materials*', '*Techniques*', as well as places to visit. It is hoped that a history of the subject may also be studied through the sections and the photographs.

In the '*Techniques*' section certain design terms, and periods of different styles have been included. So often it is presumed that these are known, and yet they are rarely listed together. Where a reader is cross-referred to another section, it is shown in capitals (e.g. *TOOLS: Embroidery frame*); if there is no reference to a section, but only to a word (in italics), then that word is in the same section. It is the author's hope that the book will show the possibilities of this most beautiful technique, whether the reader is a student, a researcher, or merely enjoys the pleasure of seeing beautiful things.

To begin a first sampler of metal thread embroidery

The following items need to be collected together. Full details are given in their relevant sections of *Tools* and *Materials*.

An embroidery frame, preferably a slate (rectangular) frame. *This is absolutely essential for metal thread embroidery.*

Backing and background fabric.

Tacking cotton, thread for sewing down the gold, pins, needles and beeswax.

Thimble, scissors, stiletto, tweezers and felt-covered board.

String, felt and card.

Metal threads: 1 reel of jap gold substitute; 1 m or length of passing thread; a length of cord; 1 dram or length of pearl purl in one size; 1 dram or length of purl in one texture and size (rough would be suitable); length of crinkle; small piece of gold leather.

Then work through the following entries in *Techniques* section: Basting, Couching, Padding, Basket filling stitch, Cord, Pearl purl, Purl, and Leather.

ARTICLES ON WHICH METAL THREAD EMBROIDERY MAY BE FOUND

CEREMONIAL

Banners Trade Unions and Livery Companies.

Ceremonial dress

Coronation trains and robes

Fukusa Cover for a lacquered box containing a ceremonial present in Japan

Gloves

Livery Companies' banners, coats of arms, an apprentice cap, Masters' crowns and funeral palls

Rank badges, Chinese

Saddle bags

Seal bags Contain the Great Seal of England, and a new one is made to hold the relevant seal of each monarch.

Tabards Sleeveless tunics decorated with heraldic devices.

DOMESTIC

Bed covers, hangings and valances Sixteenth century, early and late seventeenth century. A few from the eighteenth century, some of which are metal thread combined with quilting.

Book covers

Boxes, caskets

Cupboard carpets Early seventeenth-century hangings used to cover a cupboard.

Cushions Bible cushions, sixteenth- and seventeenth-century decorative cushions, and a few cushions for beds in the early eighteenth century.

Fire screens, pole screens

Letter cases

Panels

Paper weights

Samplers Antique ones are very rare. There is a seventeenth-century one in the Metropolitan Museum of Art, New York. Mostly second half of the twentieth century.

1 Detail of Queen Mary's coronation dress, 1911. (*Museum of London*)

Stumpwork articles Seventeenth century.

Sweet bags Sixteenth- and seventeenth-century containers for sweet-smelling herbs, placed amongst clothes and linen.

Table carpets Sixteenth and seventeenth century.

Toilet cases Seventeenth century in particular.

Towels, Turkish

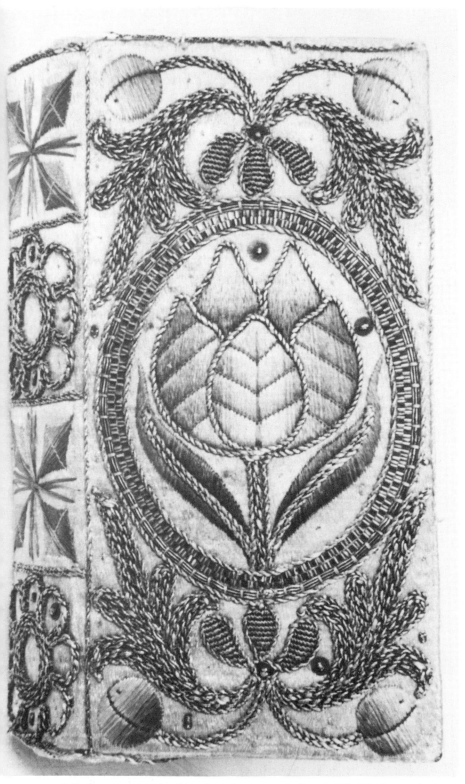

2 Book cover embroidered in coloured silks, paillettes, gold thread and foil on satin. Satin and stem stitch, with laid and couched work. (*Norfolk Museums Service: Strangers' Hall, Norwich*)

DRESS

Aprons Eighteenth-century decorative aprons.

Bags, purses

Belts

Bullfighters' outfits

Buttons

Caftans, kaftans Long, loose, coat-like garments worn in India, the Middle East and North Africa, and more recently as fashion garments.

Caps, mens' indoor Informal day caps, sixteenth, seventeenth and eighteenth century. Smoking caps, nineteenth century.

Cloaks Elizabethan.

Coats

Coifs Late sixteenth and early seventeenth century.

Collars

Cuffs

Doublets Elizabethan.

Dresses

Fans

Forehead cloths A triangular piece worn under the matching Elizabethan coif.

Gloves

Handkerchiefs Especially Elizabethan.

Jackets, women's

Kimonos

Muffs

Necklaces Second half of the twentieth century.

Parasols

Peasant costume Especially nineteenth-century Yugoslavian.

3 White satin cushion covers embroidered with silk and metal threads, then quilted. Early eighteenth century. (*Norfolk Museums Service: Strangers' Hall, Norwich*)

Pendants Second half of the twentieth century.

Petticoats Last quarter seventeenth century and the eighteenth century.

Shoes

Sleeves

Stoles

Stomachers Elizabethan, seventeenth and eighteenth century.

Trouser legs, Turkish

Trunk hose Elizabethan.

4 Embroidered velvet coat, back view. Belonged to William Pitt, 1775. (*Museum of London*)

5 Parasol cover of ivory ribbed silk embroidered in gold thread and coloured silks. Italian, mid to late seventeenth century. (*Museum of London*)

6 Man's cap and shoes, silver and silver-gilt on silk satin. Shoes with leather soles and heels. English, 1650–90. (*Burrell Collection, Glasgow Art Gallery and Museum*)

Waistcoats

Yokes

GREEK ORTHODOX CHURCH

Hierarchical vestments

Epimanika   Cuffs worn by a bishop.

Mitra   Tall rounded headdress worn by a bishop, equivalent to the western mitre.

Phelonion   Equivalent to the western chasuble.

Saccos   Tunic-like garment with wide sleeves, worn in the Middle Ages by selected patriarchs only, later by all bishops.

Priestly insignia

Epigonation   Stiffened square suspended from a bishop's girdle. Equivalent to the maniple in the western church.

Epitrachilion   Stole worn by priests and bishops.

Omophorion   Scarf-like strip decorated with applied crosses or circles, worn across the shoulders.

Orarion   Deacon's stole.

Liturgical vestments

Endyti   Equivalent to the laudian frontal of the western church.

Epitaphios sindon   A large veil decorated with the body of the crucified Christ which is carried in procession in the Good Friday services.

7 Stomacher in white satin embroidered in gold thread, trimmed with gold lace. 1660–70. (*Museum of London*)

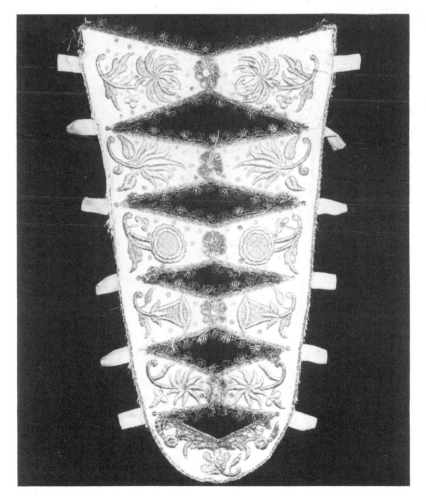

OPPOSITE
8 Motif on an omophorion. Russian, *c.* 1897. Gold plate over string. (*By kind permission of the Dean & Chapter, York Minster*)

ABOVE
9a One of a pair of desk covers on the theme of 'Choose Life' (from Deuteronomy). Silk, silk appliqué, silk and metal thread embroidery with beads and spangles. (*Kathryn Salomon, 1986. North Western Reform Synagogue*)

RIGHT
9b Detail.

Church furnishings

Podea A cloth hung below an icon, usually decorated with a scene to complement the icon.

Tomb covers They appear to have been popular in Romania and Russia in the fifteenth and sixteenth centuries. They were sometimes embroidered with the effigy of the deceased person.

JEWISH RITUAL

Jewish religious ceremonies take place in the home as well as in the synagogue, so there are a number of domestic items which are embroidered and used for religious purposes.

Atarah Decorative neckband used on the tallit (prayer shawl). A special craft called Spanier Arbeit (Spanish

10 Horse housing, 1685, belonging to the Duke of Marlborough, with the cypher of James II. (*National Army Museum, London*)

work), which developed in nineteenth- and twentieth-century Poland, was used for the atarah, for kippot, and for special chest bibs worn by brides.

Bimah cover Cover for the reader's desk.

Challah cover Napkin used to cover the challah, the plaited bread, during the ceremony of Kiddush (prayers of sanctification recited in the home before the evening meal on the eve of the Sabbath and festivals).

Chuppah Wedding canopy.

Kopporet Valance for the Ark. Used in conjunction with the parokhet. A late development, which seems to have come about as a way of covering the means of hanging the Ark curtain.

Kippah (pl. kippot) Yarmulke – skull cap.

Matzah cloth Bag with three compartments for three pieces of matzah, unleavened bread. It is used for ceremonial purposes during the Seder ser-vice, the Passover service in the home.

Parokhet (Parochet) Ark curtain, which hangs either in front of, or behind the doors of the Holy Ark. (The Ark houses the sifrei Torah, the scrolls of the Law.) The positioning of the parokhet differs according to different traditions. Sefardi Jews, who trace their ancestry back to Spain and Portugal, hang the parochet inside the Ark. Ashkenazi Jews, who trace their history back to Central and Eastern Europe, hang the parochet outside the Ark. The parochet can be a single curtain or a divided curtain. (The curtain which hung in front of the Holy of Holies in the Temple built by Herod and described by Josephus was probably a divided curtain.)

Pulpit fall Decorative panel of fabric which hangs from the reading desk.

Tallit bag Bag for the tallit (prayer shawl).

Tefillin bag Bag for the tefillin (phy-lacteries).

Torah cover Cloth which is placed over the Torah, the Scroll of the Law, in between the reading of portions of the Law.

Torah mantle Protective covering for the Torah scroll.

MILITARY

Badges

Banners, colours

Ceremonial horse furniture

Epaulettes Shoulder trimming.

Sabretaches Despatch cases worn by cavalry officers with dress uniform.

Saddle cloths, or horse housings

Uniforms

SPORT

Badges For club members or as team representatives.

Falconry equipment See *Hawking furni-ture*.

Hawking furniture Glove, pouch and hood.

WESTERN CHRISTIAN CHURCH

Alms bags Used for collecting money from the congregation at services.

Alms purses Containers for gifts of money.

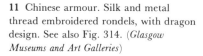

11 Chinese armour. Silk and metal thread embroidered rondels, with dragon design. See also Fig. 314. (*Glasgow Museums and Art Galleries*)

12 Green plush-covered Moroccan saddle embroidered with metal thread. (*Glasgow Museums and Art Galleries*)

Altar frontal or antependium The cloth which hangs on the front of an altar.

Apparel An embroidered strip which is fixed to the neck of the amice to fill in the gap with the chasuble, and form a standing collar.

Aumbry veil A curtain covering the aumbry, a cupboard used for the reservation of the Holy Sacrament.

Banners Used for classes or organizations within the Church, for processing and to honour sacred symbols or saints.

Book covers

Book markers

Burse, corporal case The stiffened square pocket which is made to contain the corporal and often any extra purificators. It is placed over the veiled chalice and paten on the altar, and is made in matching fabric and design to the chalice veil, stole and chasuble.

Chalice veil Referred to as the veil. A square of fabric, made to match the burse, stole and chasuble, which is used to cover the empty chalice.

Chasuble Oval-shaped vestment seamed to leave an opening in the centre which goes over the head of the celebrant at the Eucharist.

Cope A full-length semicircular cloak worn by priests and bishops when in procession or at selected services.

Corporal case See *Burse.*

Dalmatic Tunic-like vestment worn by a deacon at high celebration of the Eucharist. It matches the rest of the vestments being used.

Dossal, dorsal or dosser (back) The hanging behind an altar or a throne.

Hanging Embroidered panel of any size, used as decoration in a church.

Hearse cloth See *Pall.*

Hood of a cope Now usually represented by a flat shape, instead of the original draped fabric forming an actual hood which could be drawn up over the head.

Humeral veil A wide scarf worn round the shoulders by the officiating minister whilst holding the sacrament in procession and in the benediction of the Sacrament.

Laudian frontal or altar carpet Generally known as a throw-over frontal, being a complete covering for the top and four sides of the altar table.

Lectern fall A decorative panel of fabric that hangs down from the Bible desk, the colour of which conforms to the season of the Church year.

Maniple A short stole which hangs from the left arm as part of the Eucharistic vestments; originally a napkin. It is now rarely made as a part of new sets of vestments.

Mitre Traditional and ceremonial headdress worn by a bishop or an abbot.

OPPOSITE

13 Central motif on a green altar frontal. (*Designed by Sylvia Green and worked by Pamela Waterworth. Royal School of Church Music, Addington Palace*)

14 Banner for St John the Baptist Church, Tisbury, Wilts, *c.* 1980. (*Audrey Chorley; the Sarum Group*)

15 Cope of cloth of silver with fine French or English eighteenth-century embroidery. (*The Trustees, All Saints Chapel, Wardour Castle, Tisbury, Wiltshire*)

16 Festal Laudian altar frontal. (*Elizabeth Elvin. Royal School of Church Music, Addington Palace*)

Morse Clasp used to fasten a cope in front. Very often these are metal, but embroidered ones can be found.

Orphrey The embroidered band on an ecclesiastical vestment or hanging.

Pall (funeral), hearse cloth A large cloth placed over the coffin, casket or tomb.

Pulpit fall A decorative panel of fabric that hangs down from the reading desk in front of the pulpit, or platform, from which the sermon is delivered.

Stole A long narrow fabric band worn by clergy during services. Its colour and design will match any other vestments.

Superfrontal A strip of lace or fabric

which forms a pelmet for the altar frontal.

Tabernacle veil   A curtain covering the doors of the tabernacle, a small cupboard usually in the centre of the altar, which holds the consecrated elements of the Eucharist.

Tunicle   Short vestment worn by the subdeacon at a celebration of the Eucharist. A simple version of the dalmatic, and of a similar design to the rest of the vestments being used.

Veil   See *Chalice veil*.

17 Stole ends, part of a red set of vestments for East Coker Church. Appliqué with metal thread. (*Katarin Privett*)

TOOLS

ARI

The hook used for chain stitch embroidery in India.

AWL

A pointed instrument used by saddlers, shoemakers and all leather workers for making thread holes in leather. A stronger, sharper tool than a stiletto, with a rounded ball handle that makes it easier to use on heavy materials.

AYA TAKE DAI

See *Maru Dai.*

BEADING NEEDLES

See *Needles.*

18 Antique workbox in ebony with brass mounts, and mother-of-pearl handles to tools.

BEESWAX

See *MATERIALS: Beeswax.*

BESTIARY

Medieval handbook on natural history, the information from which inspired many of the birds and animals appearing in Opus Anglicanum designs. With the invention of printing, the woodcut illustrations became a popular embroidery design source, as may be seen from the domestic embroidery of the Elizabethan and Stuart periods in England.

BETWEEN NEEDLES

See *Needles.*

BOBBIN

Reel or spool round which thread may be wound in order to prevent it from becoming knotted. Gold threads or cords remain in good order when wound on to either a small roll of felt, or a piece of cardboard tube covered with felt. Such a roll can easily be pinned to the corner of the embroidery frame to prevent it falling to the ground and becoming unravelled as the thread is used. If jap gold is being couched as a pair of threads, it is very helpful to wind two threads together on to a bobbin, or to halve a long length, winding the two ends on to a bobbin together and leaving the folded centre of the thread to begin the work. See *Broach.*

BODKIN

Large blunt needle with a long eye, which is large enough to carry cord, ribbon or tape through a casing or holes.

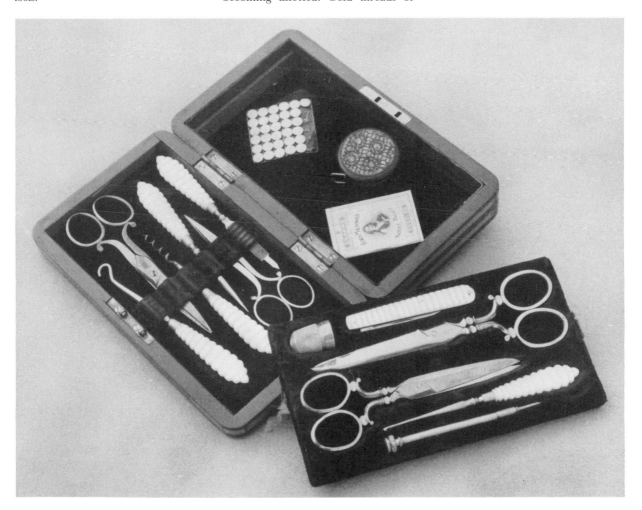

BROACH

The antique ivory or wooden spindle on to which metal thread was wound to protect it during working. Two may be seen as part of the coat of arms of the Broderers' Company. See *Bobbin*.

BURLING IRONS

Tweezers used for pulling out knots and threads whilst unpicking. An antique tool.

CALYX-EYED NEEDLES

See *Needles*.

CHAIN FORK

See *Lucet*.

CHALK

Dressmaker's (tailor's) chalk Obtainable in white and colours, shaped into thin slices for marking patterns on fabric.

Chalk pencils Of various types, for drawing out embroidery designs.

Powdered chalk Used for transferring designs by the prick and pounce method. All these chalk products are slightly greasy and so do not rub off easily. Care should be taken to use them only where they will be covered by fabric or stitching.

CHARCOAL

In powder form, is used for transferring designs by the prick and pounce method where chalk or cuttlefish would not show. A little magnesia can be added to give weight.

CHENILLE NEEDLES

See *Needles*.

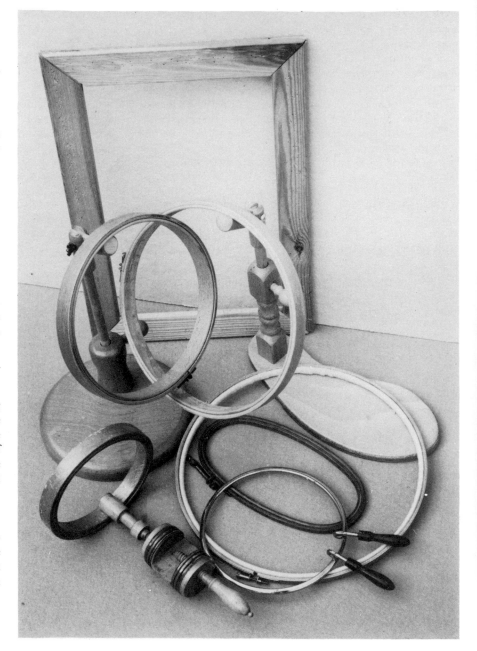

19 Cord winder.

20 A collection of frames. *Back* a stretcher, *left back* a ring frame with a table stand, *to the right* a ring frame with a fanny seat. *Left front* a ring frame with an attachment for screwing on to the table. *Right front* a larger ring frame and an oval ring frame. *Front, lying on top* a metal ring frame that springs into its other half. This is suitable for use on the sewing machine, as it is shallow in depth and so will slide under the machine foot.

CORD WINDER

A simple cord winder, to enable one to twist cords more quickly, can be made from a bent piece of firm wire, with a plastic tube covering one section, so that it is easier to hold.

CREWEL NEEDLES

See *Needles.*

CURVED NEEDLES

See *Needles.*

CUTTLE FISH

Powdered with a little magnesia added to give weight, is used as a white pounce for transferring a design to fabric. See *TECHNIQUES: Prick and Pounce.*

DARNING NEEDLES

See *Needles.*

DRAWING PINS (thumb tacks)

May be used to hold backing fabric on to a stretcher frame for working embroidery.

EGG-EYED SHARPS

See *Needles.*

EMBROIDERY FRAME

The use of a frame is essential for metal thread work, as the technique requires both hands to be free to handle the threads correctly.

Homemade frame Can be constructed from four lengths of wood of section 2·5 × 2·5 cm (1 × 1 in.), to make the rectangle. The strips are glued together, and then nailed at the corners for extra strength. For a frame of more than 46 cm (18 in.), it is advisable to strengthen each corner with a bracket.

Ring, round or hoop frame With a floor, table, seat or fanny stand, this is very useful for working small pieces which will later be applied to the main embroidery, on a large frame. A ring frame that can be adjusted by a screw attachment is more adaptable. It also allows room for the inner ring to be tightly bound with tape, completely covering the wood. This gives a much better grip to the fabric and prevents it slipping as one works. When mounting the fabric in the frame, it is the backing calico which is placed between the rings, whilst the background material, tacked to the calico within the circle made by the frame, lies freely on top of the two rings, rather than between them. This prevents any damage or marking of the background fabric. The calico backing is pulled firmly on the grain to a good even tension, and the screw on the outside ring tightened with a screwdriver.

Machine embroidery frame This is a similar ring frame, but not so deep in the hoop. This enables the frame to be slid into position without taking the foot off the machine each time. Very often these rings are made of metal and have a built-in spring to hold the fabric firm. It is essential that the fabric is drum-tight within the embroidery frame, as otherwise there will be missed and broken stitches. For working, the fabric lies flat on the machine bed and one works inside the ring.

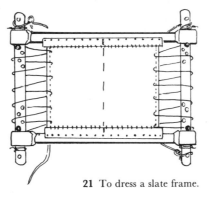

21 To dress a slate frame.

Slate frame To dress this rectangular frame, make 1 cm (½ in.) turnings on the top and bottom edges of the backing calico, and mark the centres. On the other two edges, fold the turning over a fine string and stitch into position, leaving good lengths of the string at all four ends. Mark the centre of the webbing on both rollers. With right sides together and using small overcasting stitches, work from the centres outwards to attach the webbing on the rollers to the top and bottom edges of the backing calico. Roll surplus fabric on to a roller, slot in the side pieces of the frame, and peg to hold fabric tight. Tie off the four ends of string tight to the frame; then, using a large-eyed needle, lace the sides to the frame with a fine string. Knot the ends around the corners; the tension can then be adjusted as required. The background fabric is tacked (basted) on to the backing calico, and the two are tightened up together to be the same tension. (See *TECHNIQUES: Basting, Tacking.*) The tension of the frame should not be drum-tight for metal thread, as this can result in ugly puckering when the embroidery is taken off the frame. The tension should be firm but *not* taut.

Stretcher frame This can be bought from an art shop in pairs of lengths of wood, so that any size of rectangle can be made up as required. The mitred corners slot in together, and make a good firm frame, an advantage being that the sides will also dismantle easily for storage. The disadvantage to this type of frame is that the backing calico is attached with drawing pins, which have to be removed and replaced to tighten up the tension of the calico during working.

EMERY CUSHION

A small pin cushion filled with emery powder. A rusty or rough needle can be drawn through the cushion to restore the surface.

FELT-COVERED BOARD

Of dimensions approximately 15 × 10 cm (6 × 4 in.), this makes a good cutting board when working with purls. The texture of the felt prevents the cut purls from rolling and jumping about when a second length is being cut to size.

FELT ROLL

See *Bobbin.*

FRAME

See *Embroidery frame.*

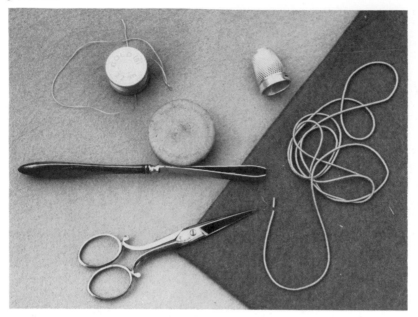

22 Felt board with purl ready for cutting to the required length with small sharp scissors. Tweezers, beeswax, thimble and thread are alongside.

GLOVING NEEDLES
See *Needles*.

HANDGUARD
A piece of lawn, linen or cotton used to lay over the part of the embroidery which is not being worked on, so that it is not rubbed by the hand or arm of the worker. A large rectangle may be laid over the whole frame with just a hole cut out to reveal the area being worked. In the eighteenth century this would have been made of paper or parchment.

HERBALS
Books with illustrations of plant life which provided many an Elizabethan needlewoman's inspiration for the garden and country flowers incorporated in the scrolling designs of the period. Because of the demand for the herbals for this use, the French and Italians produced drawings and pattern books especially for the use of the English needlewoman.

HOMEMADE FRAME
See *Embroidery frame*.

HOOP
See *Embroidery frame*.

KAKU DAI
See *Maru dai*.

LUCET (chain fork)
Traditionally, a tool of bone, ivory or wood used for making cords. The weight of thread used to make this square-sectioned cord can vary from the very fine up to a medium-weight string.

23 Lucet.

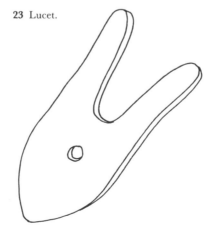

MACHINE EMBROIDERY FRAME
See *Embroidery frame*.

MARU DAI
Maru means round and *dai* means device. The Maru is one of ten or so pieces of hand-manipulated devices that are used in Japan to make braids. There are three other pieces that are in general use: *Kaku dai*, meaning square device, *Aya take dai*, meaning low device, and *Taka dai*, meaning high device. There are many schools of braiding in Japan and over a long period of time each has developed braiding equipment to its own preferred design. There are no standard 'right designs'. (Information provided by Roderick Owen.)

MELLORE
A traditional metal tool with one sharp-pointed end which replaces the need for a stiletto, and the other end a rounded spatula shape used for pushing and manipulating the metal threads into position. This tool is still used by embroiderers in the professional workrooms making naval and military regalia. The amateur embroiderer manages with a stiletto and a pair of eyebrow tweezers.

NEEDLES
An assortment is needed. Check that the eye of the selected needle is smooth and will not rub the thread.

Sharps Commonly used for plain sewing, sharps are a normal-length needle with a small eye. Assorted sizes 5–10 are recommended.

Egg-eyed sharps The traditional needle for metal passing thread, but are unfortunately no longer manufactured.

Betweens A short edition of sharps, these are lovely to work with, and are known as the 'tailor's needle'. Experts sew more quickly with a short needle. Assorted sizes 5–10 are recommended.

Straws Known as the 'milliner's needle', these are a longer edition of sharps. A good needle to travel easily

through layers of padding. Assorted sizes 5–10.

Crewel These needles are made for embroidery. They are the same length and thickness as sharps, but have a large eye to carry the various threads used. Nos. 8 and 9 are useful sizes.

Tapestry Needles made for embroidery on canvas. They have blunt points and are needed for composite stitches,

24 A Japanese braid making stool.

25 Pendant, made using handmade braid and cord. (*Eunice Wells*)

26 Mellore.

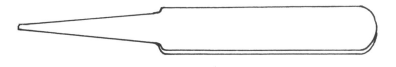

lacing and surface darning. Sizes 20–24 are suitable for average work.

Chenille These have extremely large eyes and sharp points. They take thick yarns, and will carry metal threads and the smaller cords through the fabric for finishing off, to avoid using the sling method. Sizes 20 and 22 are useful.

Darners and long darners Can be of great use for soft sculpture where length of needle is required. Assorted sizes 16–3 for thick material.

Beading needles Long and extremely fine so that they can pass through the smallest bead or piece of cut purl.

Curved needles Used in upholstery and construction of articles decorated with embroidery, e.g. boxes, burses and toys. They are rarely used in connection with metal thread techniques, but can be very helpful for applying heavily padded areas or for completing the sides of raised sections.

Gloving needles These are made with a cutting edge to pass easily through leather. They make too large a hole for embroidery purposes, and an ordinary short fine sewing needle gives much better results.

Calyx-eyed needles Self-threading needles with a fine slit at the top of the eye through which the thread is forced.

Sewing machine needles These are manufactured to suit each make of machine. They are available in all sizes to complement the weight of fabric and thread. Some manufacturers have produced a large needle to carry the heavier yarns that embroiderers may wish to use in their machines, but many of the textured yarns still have to be wound on to the bobbin, and the work stitched from the wrong side. Some sewing machines can carry twin needles for special effects.

PARCHMENT
See *Vellum*.

PEGS
The metal or wooden pegs which are required to hold a slate frame in shape, and at the necessary tension, whilst the embroidery is being worked.

POUNCE
The powdered charcoal, chalk or cuttlefish used for transferring designs in the prick and pounce method. See *TECHNIQUES: Transference of design.*

POUNCE PAD (Pouncer)
A small roll of felt, sewn up to stop it coming undone, which is used to apply the pounce for the prick and pounce method of transferring a design.

PRICKER
Used for making tiny holes in the paper pattern for the prick and pounce method of transferring a design to fabric. These could be very decorative tools and can be found as part of antique sewing boxes. Today's substitute is a needle with the eye end pushed into a cork to provide a handle.

RING FRAME
See *Embroidery frame*.

ROLLERS
See *Emboidery frame (Slate frame)*.

ROUND FRAME
See *Embroidery frame*.

SCISSORS

Dressmaking shears For cutting out fabric.

Small strong scissors With firm points for cutting the metal threads.

Embroidery scissors Very small with fine thin pointed blades for trimming appliqué and cut work, and getting a fine cut finish on thread or fabric.

Paper scissors As paper is notorious for blunting scissors, it is advisable to keep a pair exclusively for the purpose.

Pinking scissors These give a regular zig-zag cut edge that can help prevent fraying, or be used decoratively.

SCREW
An ordinary carpenter's wood screw, sized as appropriate, is used for crimping plate. The narrow flat strip of metal is pressed along the ridges of the screw to give a textured surface.

SEWING MACHINE
With the adaptability of the modern machine and the marvellous range of metallic thread manufactured for machine embroidery, the sewing machine can make an important contribution to metal thread embroidery of all types and for all purposes. It does take time and practice to appreciate the possibilities, but exciting results have opened up a new side to the technique.

SEWING MACHINE NEEDLES
See *Needles*.

SHEARS
See *Scissors*.

SHARP NEEDLES
See *Needles*.

SLATE FRAME
See *Embroidery frame*.

SLIP
Motif of a flower which includes its foliage, stem, and 'heel', where it has been torn from the plant. Sometimes it may include a small section of the root system. A 'slip' is a term still used by gardeners for a cutting used for reproducing the plant. Slips were predominant in designs of the sixteenth and seventeenth centuries, often being worked separately, and then applied to the main article.

STILETTO
A very sharp pointed steel instrument used for making holes for taking the larger threads and cords through to the back of the work from the right side. The hole is always made from the right side. The advantage of the stiletto is that the sharp point travels between the threads, then as the shaft of the instrument widens, it forces the

threads apart without breaking them. They will return to their original position hugging the thread that is passed through the hole, leaving no raw broken threads.

STRAW NEEDLES
See *Needles.*

STRETCHER FRAME
See *Embroidery frame.*

STYLUS
See *Stiletto.*

TAKA DAI
See *Maru dai.*

TAPE MEASURE
It is important to remember that with wear a linen tape will stretch, so that for really accurate measurement a steel tape, or wooden or metal rule is essential.

TAPESTRY NEEDLES
See *Needles.*

TEMPLATE
A paper, card or parchment shape which can be drawn, painted or stitched around to give a design line.

THIMBLE
A protective covering for the finger, usually worn on the second finger of the hand guiding the needle. When working on an embroidery frame, with one hand handling the needle above the frame, and the other hand below the frame, it may be found advantageous to wear a thimble on the second finger of each hand.

THUMB TACKS
See *Drawing pins.*

27 Tracing wheel.

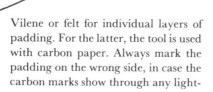

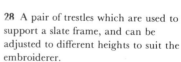

TRACING WHEEL
This dressmaker's tool, which comes in several sizes, can save a great deal of time when several duplicate paper patterns need to be traced for various areas of a design, or for marking up

Vilene or felt for individual layers of padding. For the latter, the tool is used with carbon paper. Always mark the padding on the wrong side, in case the carbon marks show through any light-

28 A pair of trestles which are used to support a slate frame, and can be adjusted to different heights to suit the embroiderer.

coloured or fine fabric being used on top of the padded area. The tracing wheel should not be used on the actual background fabric, as the sharp prickers on the wheel can damage the fabric.

TRESTLES
The pair of supports which hold a slate frame for working. Although a slate frame may be balanced between two tables or other articles of furniture, it is much more convenient for

the embroiderer to use trestles which can be adjusted to a convenient height. This prevents back problems and aching shoulders.

TWEEZERS

Used for picking up sections of cut purl, and manipulating metal threads round corners. Threads can be squeezed to accentuate a sharp angle or to take on required shapes.

VELLUM

A good-quality parchment. As it was stiff enough to hold its shape, with firm edges, it was used by embroiderers in the past for padding areas of gold work. It gave much the same result as today's use of thin card to pad shapes that require a flat, smooth, crisp finish.

MATERIALS

ACID-FREE TISSUE PAPER

Commercially available tissue, generally used for wrapping and interleaving where a degree of purity is necessary.

ADMIRALTY GOLD

Refers to the quality (by metal content) that the Admiralty requires for the threads and purls used on the Service's uniforms.

AIGUILLETTE

Used in connection with embroidery, refers to a spangle or decorative metal piece that can be incorporated into the design.

ALUMINIUM TWIST

A modern metal thread available in several weights, which is untarnishable. It does not reflect as much light as a silver or silver lurex thread due to its slightly blue grey colour.

ANTIQUE METAL THREAD

The 'antique' refers to the colour of the thread, which is a dark-toned aluminium, copper, gold or silver. Very often silver or gold thread is spun or twisted with black to give the effect. It is invaluable for adding depth and variation, and for throwing up the brighter areas of the design. (*See Fig. 31.*)

ARTIFICIAL PEARLS

These have been made since the mid-seventeenth century, when they were extensively produced for embroidery on dress. They have the advantage over real pearls of keeping their colour and of being much less expensive. Since plastic 'pearls' became available at an even lower cost, it has been

29 Complete crown and one in progress. Worn by Keeper of the Jewel House, Tower of London. (*Hobson & Sons (London) Ltd*)

30 Collar, officer of field rank, Household Cavalry. (*Hobson & Sons (London) Ltd*)

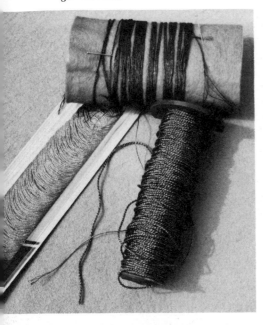

possible to experiment with painting, spraying and dyeing them to suit the requirements of the embroidery.

AURIPHRYGIUM

A term referring to gold fringe or metal thread embroidery. See *TECHNIQUES.*

AURUM BATTUTUM

Gold beaten into a very fine sheet and cut into narrow strips. This could then be woven into fabric, plaited into braids or wound round a silk thread core to make a gold thread for couching. This last was used to make St Cuthbert's stole at Durham Cathedral (*c.* AD 909–916). By the time of the great period of Opus Anglicanum (1250–1350) the gold thread was in fact silver gilt, and no longer aurum battutum.

AURUM FILATUM ROMANI

The gold thread which was imported to Europe from Byzantium. It was of

31 Various antique gold threads.

32 Fine, flat narrow gold strips (*aurum battutum*) which had been woven with wool into braids of two widths. From the Taplow Burial, Bucks, AD 600. (*Reproduced by courtesy of the Trustees of the British Museum*)

33 St Cuthbert's stole, showing the Prophet Jonah. (*By kind permission of the Dean and Chapter, Durham Cathedral*)

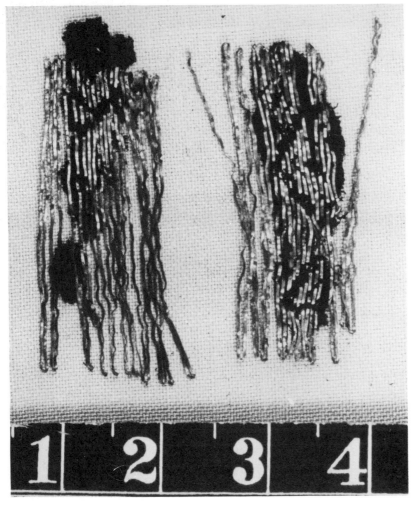

34 Lenten altar frontal with tie-and-dye background, for St Mary's and All Saints', Ellingham. (*Midge Burnett*)

better quality than the similar type called 'Cyprus gold', as the strips of animal membrane wound round the core were of greater width and had heavier gilding. The core, too, was almost exclusively of yellow silk.

BACKGROUND FABRIC

For traditional goldwork, the background needs to be closely woven without too much texture, which can distort the evenness and direction of the couched threads. Once the embroiderer can handle metal threads to good effect, almost any fabric can be used. Because of the weight of metal thread, and the necessity of using a frame for this technique, a backing of calico or linen is nearly always used. This adds the necessary strength and quality to the ground fabric, giving the embroiderer control on a fabric that, used on its own, might be too loosely woven, soft or thin.

Metal thread motifs can always be worked on calico or linen, then applied to the ground fabric, should that fabric be unsuitable for working direct. Brocades, damasks, and patterned fabrics are the least successful for metal thread work, as they restrict the embroidery design to merely enriching what is already there.

Silks are the ideal choice, as the sheen is a perfect foil for metal threads. It entirely depends, however, on the design and quality desired. The following list suggests fabrics which have been successfully used with this technique, though it must be pointed out that natural fibres are far nicer to handle than man-made: bourette or noil, calico, duchesse satin used on the right or wrong side, flannel of all types, georgette, grosgrain, lamé, linen of all types, lurex, moiré, net, non-woven fabrics, nun's veiling, organdie, organza (shot or plain), scrim, shantung, shot silk, taffeta, Thai silk, Tussah silk, velvet and velveteens plain, corded, embossed and panne (see *TECHNIQUES: Velvet*) and Viyella, which is one of the nicest surfaces to work on. Obviously, very fine transparent fabrics can carry only the finest of metal threads.

It is well worth running a needle through the fabric you plan to use, as some of the thick grosgrains, moirés etc. are very stiff, and though they look beautiful, they can be hard work to stitch into.

BACKING FABRIC
Usually a calico or linen, the weight of which depends on how much support the background fabric requires, the amount of metal thread embroidery that will need support, and the use to which the completed piece will be put.

BADLA
An Indian silver and silver-gilt metal thread made of a loosely coiled wire, similar to a coarse check purl.

BATTU
Eighteenth-century flattened wire of very thin gold, which has been passed through rollers; similar to tinsel.

BAUDERKIN
A rich fabric of the Middle Ages, woven in silk and gold threads of a damask type.

BEADS
Small balls, cylinders or other shapes which, having a hole through their centres, may be strung together as a length, or sewn individually on to a background, either massed together for texture or placed to form patterns. They may be made of porcelain, glass, wood, steel, plastic, stone, or other natural materials. They may be dyed, painted, enamelled, and given a wide variety of coloured or metallic finishes. See *TECHNIQUES: Beading*

Rocailles The trade name for the

transparent glass beads used for general embroidery.

Round rocailles (seed beads) Round beads with round holes.

Square rocailles (toscas) Round beads with square holes.

Charlottes Beads faceted on the outside.

Bugle beads Small glass or plastic cylinders, round or faceted in section, coming in all colours, transparent or opaque, and in metallic finishes. They can vary in length from $\frac{1}{10}$ in. to $2\frac{1}{2}$ or 3 in. (4 mm to 6 or 8 cm) for those that were used for the 1920s fashion fringes. Because of their rigid shape, they are useful in certain areas of design using geometric motives, or to give a contrast in texture to the softer reflection of beads or massed metal threads.

Pound beads Transparent glass beads

35 Detail of Indian mat, showing beetle wings incorporated with couched metal threads. Late nineteenth to early twentieth century. (*Embroiderers' Guild Collection*)

which were dyed in a wide range of colours, and imported from Italy and Germany in the nineteenth century. Their name comes from the fact that they were sold by weight.

BEESWAX
The thread used for couching metal threads and for sewing on beads, braids, cords and leather should be passed over the surface of a piece of beeswax to coat the fibres. This smooths, stiffens and strengthens the thread to give it longer life. It also helps to prevent it knotting whilst being worked.

BEETLE WINGS

In the nineteenth century the dark, iridescent wings of beetles were incorporated in embroidery to make rich patterns. A small hole was made at each end of the wing so that it might be attached to the fabric. The technique was fashionable in America and Britain, and may well have originated in India, where they were much used.

BONDINA/BONDAWEB

Where a soft fabric, that frays and is difficult to handle, is being applied to a background fabric before the embroidery is started, it may be helpful to use a bonding agent. This can be bought by the yard or piece, and should have the required shape traced on to the paper backing, wrong side up. The Bondina is then cut out, with

36 Indian hat of red cotton covered with metal thread, gold beads, tinsel and beetle wings. Such hats evolved from the small cap worn under the turban and are associated with informal dress. (*By courtesy of the Trustees of the Victoria & Albert Museum*)

small turning allowances, and ironed on to the back of the fabric to be applied. The shape is cut out through the paper backing, the Bondina and the fabric. This assures that no fraying takes place. Next the paper is peeled away, leaving the bonding agent on the back of the piece of fabric to be applied. As it is stiffened slightly, the fabric is now quite easy to handle. The cut-out shape is ironed into position on the background fabric, and is then ready to have the raw edges treated. When the bonding agent is first ironed on to the shape to be applied, and the paper is still in position, wrinkling may take place on the fabric, but this corrects itself as soon as the paper is peeled off. If the Bondina does not appear to have stuck to the fabric completely, then a hotter iron should be used. The use of a steam iron can be helpful on thicker fabric, and to avoid scorching.

BOURGETTE (Noil)

Fabric woven from yarn that is spun from the waste produced in the manufacture of schappe silk. The small, irregular lumps give it its character. See *Background fabric*.

BRAIDS

Flat decorative braids are available in metal threads, but with far less choice than in previous decades owing to their high cost. A number are produced in Lurex threads, but their bright tinsel appearance makes them difficult to incorporate with metal thread embroidery. Russia braid is one of the traditional braids that retains its popularity.

Handmade braid and cords It is now possible to learn this skill from teachers who have brought the techniques from Peru and Japan. Metallic couching threads can be made up into individually designed braids and cords. By mixing variegated coloured metal threads, coloured silks, and other yarns a wide selection of sizes and designs can be made to suit any piece of work. Japanese pattern books are available in this country and the possi-

37 Officer's uniform, 1890. Westmorland and Cumberland Yeomanry. Detail of sleeve with metal Russia braid, cord, a flat braid, and fur cuff and trimmings. (*National Army Museum, London*)

bilities are endless. See *TECH-NIQUES*.

BRASS WASHERS

Washers and other pieces of metal or 'found objects', as they were known, were incorporated into metal thread embroidery in the 1960s and early 1970s. They added a variation of shape and texture to the available threads, and influenced the design quality of the period. Washers can make a very good padding under leather or threads, giving a strong firm shape.

BRIGHT PURL

See *Purl*.

BROCADE

A richly figured woven silk cloth, sometimes incorporating metal threads. See *Background fabric*.

38 White Spitalfields silk, brocaded using a flat silver thread. Many of the silver strips in the background have cut through the other silk threads, and so have had to be couched to restore this fine example of the weaver's skill in using metal threads. Worn by Ann Fanshawe, 1752–3. (*Museum of London*)

39a Green velvet cope, raised work with gold thread over vellum. Probably made in France, restored in China. Early nineteenth century. (*St John the Baptist's Church, Tisbury, Wiltshire*)

BUGLE BEADS
See *Beads*.

BULLION
The name given to the larger-sized purls when described in mass, or by weight. It is more often seen used on military or naval insignia, or the larger heraldic devices. Hence the name 'bullion embroidery' which is given to the heavy formal metal thread work used on military and official regalia.

CALICO
In embroiderers' terminology, the natural unbleached cotton which comes in a variety of weights and widths, and is ideal as a backing fabric for any work done on a frame, as well as for certain interlinings. During the 1980s it has become popular as a background fabric owing to its pleasant colour, and because it is so nice to handle. See *Backing fabric*.

CANNETILLE
A disused name for purl, and also for a twisted braid, made in either gold or silver.

CANVAS
A fabric made from cotton, hemp, jute or linen in a lattice-like, loosely woven stiffened cloth with a range of numbers of threads to the inch. Through the ages metal threads have occasionally been combined with silk or wool in canvas work (also referred to as needlepoint and tapestry). In the last half of the 1980s exciting work is

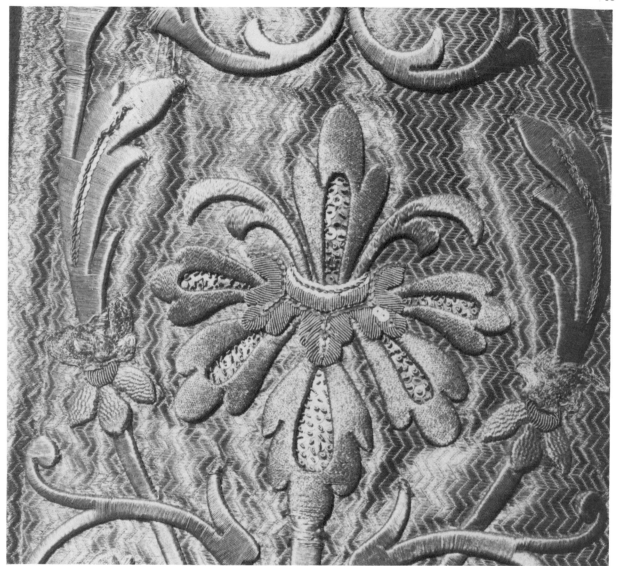

39b Detail.

being done in metal threads on single canvas with the sewing machine. It is possible to work the traditional canvas work stitches with the more pliable and stronger metallic-type threads now being produced, whereas metal threads would never previously have stood up to the wear of being pulled through the stiff threads of the canvas. See *TECHNIQUES: Canvas*.

CARD
Card with a smooth finish and cleanly cut edges may be used for padding.

Firm, strong card is also used for mounting finished work which needs a taut backing, such as panels, boxes etc.

CARTISANE
The thin parchment or vellum that was used to pad the raised areas in the guipure laces and braids of the sixteenth century, and later for embroidered motifs on items of dress and ecclesiastical furnishings and vestments. The raised area was covered with a very fine gold or silver passing thread, or coloured silk yarn. See *TECHNIQUES: Guimped embroidery* and *Padding*.

CHARLOTTES
See *Beads*.

CHECK
The manufacturers' name for what is commonly known as crinkle, so crinkle may sometimes be bought under this title.

CHECK PURL
See *Purl*.

CHENILLE THREAD
A velvet-type thread, taking its name from the French *chenille*, meaning 'caterpillar'. It can give an interesting change of texture and colour to metal

thread when couched alongside, or within an area of metal threads. It was probably not invented before 1700, though a darned silk pile (mosswork?) is often mistaken for it in earlier work.

CLOTH OF GOLD/SILVER

A rich fabric woven with silk and gold or silver threads. Nowadays there are many manmade gold or silver lamés, lurex, tissues, jerseys, nets and other fancy fabrics obtainable. They vary in quality and tone of colour, but there is one to suit every purpose.

COPPER THREADS

Now much more readily available, these come in many of the same types as the gold and silver metal threads, both the traditional types and the modern yarns. At the end of the 1980s, however, a jap copper has not yet been imported. Available are fine cords, couching threads, knitting yarns, lurex threads, machine embroidery threads, metallic coloured yarns, passing threads, pearl purl and purls.

CORD

A rounded length of threads, of any type, that have been twisted or plaited in a decorative manner, to make a trimming suitable for couching on to a required line. The heavier weight of a cord compared to a single thread adds an interesting variation to metal thread embroidery. Metal thread cords are available in different weights, depending on how many groups of threads are twisted together. There is also a variation of quality and texture.

Grecian cord Made up of groups of threads that give a striped finish; bright alternating with a rough or textured surface.

Gold crepe As its name suggests, has a matt gold finish.

Twist A type of plaited cord, which gives a more textured finish than the more usual smoothly twisted cords. This heavier 'twist' is available in several sizes. See *Braid* for handmade braid and cords; also *TECHNIQUES: Cord laying.*

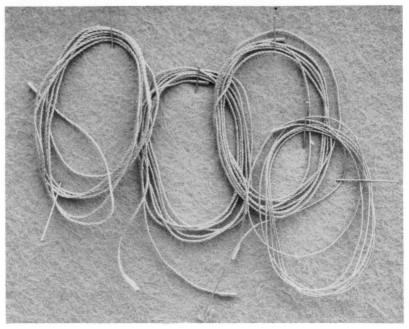

40 Four sizes of twist.

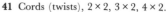

41 Cords (twists), 2 × 2, 3 × 2, 4 × 2.

CORDONNET

Used to refer in the eighteenth century to a fine silk cord used for making chainstitched and Indian-style embroidery. In the 1970s, a fine metal passing thread in a variety of golds, silvers and coppers was produced with this name.

COTTON

A fluffy vegetable fibre which grows from the seed pod of the cotton flower. There are three basic types of cotton fibre, and each type can be converted to specific end uses: (1) coarse, short and dull with up to 2 cm ($\frac{3}{4}$ in.) long staple; (2) medium quality with up to 3 cm ($1\frac{1}{4}$ in.) long staple;

12 Cords (twists), 2 × 2 × 2, 3 × 2 × 2, 4 × 2 × 2.

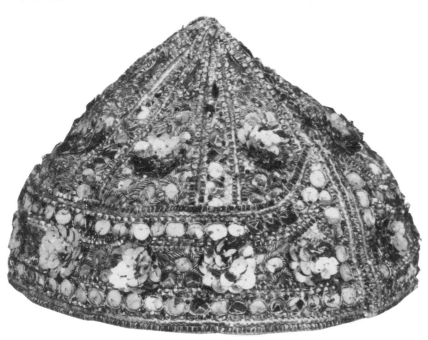

43 Indian hat of red cotton covered with sequins, metal thread, tinsel and glass beads. Hyderabad, mid nineteenth century. (*By courtesy of the Trustees of the Victoria & Albert Museum*)

clydella, corduroy, denim, organdie and velveteen. See *Background fabric.*

COTON PERLE

Pearl cotton is a two-ply twisted silk-like thread, made in four weights: 12, 8, 5 and 3 (fine to heavy). It has a high gloss and is made in a good range of colours. This thread has many uses when combined with metal threads, both as a yarn to stitch with, and as one to be couched.

COUCHING THREADS

Threads that are sewn on to the background fabric by a separate finer thread, either because they are too thick to pull through the ground fabric, would disintegrate very quickly if sewn with, or are too rare or expensive to waste on the underside of the embroidery.

CRINKLE (Check)

A gold or silver fine twist with a central core, made in three sizes. It has a crimped finish, which gives an undulating line, making an interesting change of texture when couched alongside smoother threads. (*See Fig. 44.*)

CYPRUS GOLD

Cyprus gold (Sipers gold, Aurum Filatum Cyprese, or Cypriot gold thread) was first used in the eleventh century, and was carried to Europe by Levantine traders down to late medieval times. In the beginning it was made of a narrow strip of animal gut burnished with gold leaf, wound spirally around a fine core of cotton, linen or silk thread. They were probably wound together in a moist state, as historical samples prove difficult to separate from each other. With a gold thread the core was usually dyed yellow or red, while with silver it was left white. This inexpensive, lightweight flexible thread, sometimes known as 'skin gold' or 'membrane gold', was very popular. But it was less durable, the gold rubbed off more easily, and it had an inferior lustre to the genuine gold thread. This thread was used extensively for textiles, but it is doubtful whether it was used for embroidery

(3) the best quality, fine, high-lustre fibre with up to 6·5 cm (2½ in.) long staple. Cotton is spun into different weights of yarn, then woven, and can be finished in about seventy different variations. The types most useful to the metal thread embroiderer as a background fabric are calico, canvas (though a linen canvas is preferable),

44 Three sizes of crinkle.

because of the technical problems. The Cyprus gold thread, imported through Cyprus in the Middle Ages, which is mentioned in fifteenth-century inventories, was considered to be the best and purest metal thread, and laws were passed about the acceptable standard of the gold to prevent it being mixed with Laten de Spayne, an alloy from Spain. See *Gilt-leather thread.*

DAMASCENE (DAMASK) GOLD
A gold thread, most likely silver gilt, mentioned in Tudor inventories. It was probably named after the place of export, Damascus, rather than the area where it was made.

DOWLAS
A firm linen fabric traditionally used as an interlining for church work.

FABRIC
Metal thread embroidered motives can be applied to any fabric so long as it is strong enough to support the weight of the embroidery. The choice depends on the design and fashion feel of the day. See *Background fabric.*

FABRIC PROTECTION
See *Spray fabric protector.*

FELT
Usually made by compressing woollen fibres together so that they are perma-nently entangled. Being non-fraying and of a reasonable thickness that hardly compresses, felt makes an ideal padding, either singly or in layers, for metal thread embroidery, or to enrich areas of leather. When padding areas to be covered with metal threads, it is advisable to use a felt of a colour as near to the thread as possible.

Handmade felt In the last decade there has been a great interest in pro-ducing one's own variegated and tex-tured homemade felts, and a number of articles have been written on the methods that may be used in the home. With the right selection and an embroidery design which builds from the background, there are possibilities for interesting experiments to be worked in metal thread on this type of ground fabric.

FILO FLOSS (Filo silk)
A two-ply, loosely twisted pure silk thread. It needs considerable skill to use it well, as it is very easily snagged and roughened. The wide choice of subtle colours and the nature of the silk make it ideal for long-and-short stitch, where the blending of the col-ours, or 'painting with threads' is the sought-after effect.

FILOSELLE
A stranded pure silk thread made from the waste products of the silk worm. It was cheaper than filo floss,

and much easier to handle, but is now unobtainable.

FLANNEL
Traditionally a soft, woollen cloth that is loosely woven. Nowadays there is considerable difference in the weight and texture of the cloth; some is woven with a twill weave and napped on both sides. It is this closely woven, smoother-finished cloth which can make a lovely background fabric for metal thread embroidery. See *Background fabric.*

FLOSS SILK (Sleave silk, Sleided silk)
Made from the soft external covering of silkworm cocoons, it is a raw untwisted yarn which can be split down into very find threads. It gives excellent results for long-and-short stitch, laid work and other occasions where the threads need to blend together to give a smooth finish. It was almost the only kind of silk available during the period of Opus Anglica-num, and was ideal for the split stitch favoured by the ecclesiastical embroi-derers of the time. A few fine fila-ments were used to work the faces, whilst a thicker yarn was used to embroider the draperies of the many religious figures that decorated vest-ments and furnishings. Floss silk is no longer available.

FOUNDATION FABRIC
The calico or linen that is stretched on a frame, to carry the background fab-ric for the embroidery. See *Backing fabric.*

FRENCH CHALK
A powdered chalk that can lift grease marks off a fabric. It should be sprin-kled on to the area, allowed to stay in position long enough to absorb the grease, then shaken or brushed off. It can also be used for the prick and pounce method of transferring a de-sign to fabric. See *TECHNIQUES: Prick and pounce.*

FRINGE
Originally a method of neatening off

45 Chinese rank badge. First rank military – unicorn, late nineteenth century. Embroidered with floss silks, silver and silver-gilt wire threads, wound round a silk core. Long-and-short stitch with laid and couched work. Applied coral beads. (*Embroiderers' Guild Collection*)

the raw edge of fabric, and of adding decoration at the same time, by plaiting and knotting the ends of the warp threads and leaving them to hang free. This developed into a separate manufactured border composed of silken or metal threads, and when fashion ordained, beads were used for the fringe. Gold bullion fringe can be seen on military and naval dress uniforms. Metal threads fringes were very popular with the ecclesiastical embroiderers of the nineteenth and early twentieth centuries.

FRISON
Eighteenth-century embroidery was sometimes trimmed with a textured wire which was the equivalent of a purl or spiral wire flattened on rollers.

FRISURE
A matt gold wire of the eighteenth century which was coiled round a large needle and treated as purl. Being a heavier thickness, it was used for the centre of flowers.

FRIZE
A flattened copper wire that has been electroplated to give it a gold, silver or other coloured surface, wound round a square mould to form a coarser type of purl. It is then cut into short lengths and sewn on like a bead.

GEORGETTE
A lightweight sheer fabric with a fine textured matt surface and a crêpe finish. It is strong enough to carry lightweight metal thread and bead embroidery for a fashion garment. See *Background fabric*.

GILT LEATHER THREAD
Gilt or silver-gilt and silver leather strips were used by the Chinese weavers in their brocades up until late medieval times, when this technique was replaced by strips of gilt mulberry paper, also used as flat threads. Occasionally these silver-gilt paper strips were wrapped around a silk or cotton core. The gilt leather strips were used as untwisted weft in silk fabrics, and

their asymmetric patterns had a major influence on the new Italian 'gothic'-style designs when the brocades made their appearance in Europe at the beginning of the fourteenth century. Many of these brocades were made in China for Mohammedan countries and bear Islamic inscriptions. The Mongol conquest of Persia and the establishment of Mongol dynasties after 1230 led to the gilt leather techniques being used in Persian brocades. European weavers did not take up the practice of using either gilt leather or gilt paper strips, but continued to use the finer membrane gold, which was much suppler, so the use of gilt leather does indicate a Far Eastern origin. See *Cyprus gold*.

GIMP
Referred to by an embroiderer, means a narrow braid with a stiffened base.

GOLD THREADS
Both traditional gold threads and those produced by technology are available to the embroiderer. See details under *Bullion, Crinkle, Frize, Imitation jap gold, Jap gold, Jap gold substitute, Knitting yarns, Lurex, Machine embroidery thread, Metallic coloured yarns, Passing thread, Pearl purl, Plate, Purls, Tambour, Twists;* and *TECHNIQUES*.

GREASEPROOF PAPER
A cheap alternative to tracing paper, which can be used for transferring designs to fabric.

GROSGRAIN
A heavy silk cloth with a ribbed effect. See *Background fabric*.

GROUND FABRIC
See *Background fabric*.

GUIPURE
A term used in cut work, open work, and lace. In metal thread embroidery it refers to heavy wired metal lace, or certain edges worked with metal threads.

HAIR
Very few examples of human hair

46 'Opus I'. (*Ann Sutton*)

47 Single French glove, *c.* 1600. Detail of cuff embroidered with silver and hair on white satin. (*Spence Collection, Museum of London*)

used as an embroidery thread, with metal thread, are in existence. Its use enables a finely drawn line to be worked, and may be seen in the 'drawings' which were popular in the late eighteenth and early nineteenth century, but no gold work was involved.

HANDMADE BRAID
See *Braid*.

HANDMADE PAPER
Paper making has now become an absorbing addition to the embroiderer's skills, requiring little more than

48 'Circle of figures'. Couching and long-and-short stitch, with some gold thread couched. Gold in the Japanese paper background. Diameter 91 cm (36 in.). (*Margaret Hall*)

kitchen equipment and supplies from the local hardware store. With the addition of off-cuts of threads, fabrics, ribbons, different papers, flower petals, small leaves, grasses, dyes, paints or inks, some interesting backgrounds can be made. Backed with calico, the paper is certainly strong enough to carry metal thread em-

broidery worked by hand or machine.

HORSETAIL SILK (Maltese silk)

A fine, strong silk used to couch metal threads. Unfortunately, this is no longer on the market. It was originally available in skeins, which were plaited and hung from a peg on the embroidery frame; thus the term 'horsetail' evolved in the workrooms.

IMITATION JAP GOLD THREAD

Originally manufactured as an alter-

native to jap gold. It is now made in four weights and is very much easier to handle than the original jap gold or the presently available jap gold substitute. Originally it had a real gold content, but when in recent years this specification became so expensive, the manufacturers changed over to a metallized polyester. It does not tarnish. Also available in silver in three sizes. (*See Fig. 49.*)

INVISIBLE NYLON THREAD

Made in a clear white and a transparent darker shade. Its advantage is

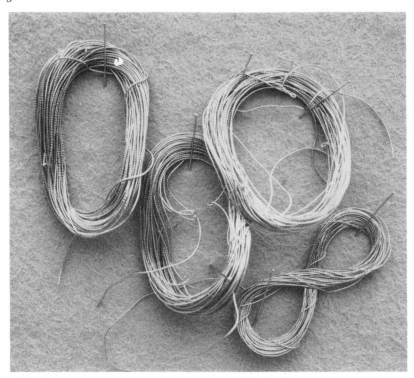

49 Imitation jap gold.

ABOVE RIGHT
50 Jap gold, no longer available in the shops.

51 Jap gold substitute. 1K, 2K, 3K, 4K.

that, being almost invisible, it does not break up the reflective quality of metal threads, cords or braids as they are couched down. The disadvantages are that it takes practice to handle it with ease and that it is difficult to see where one has sewn! To prevent the thread from knotting in use, it is helpful to wax it. The thread is also liable to slide out of the eye of the needle, so it can be knotted in without affecting the stitching. Being nylon the thread does stretch, so it needs to be handled with a firm tension and a backstitch worked every fourth or fifth stitch to prevent it slipping, thus allowing the couched thread to become loose.

JACERON
Pearl purl (American).

JAP GOLD (Japanese gold)
Gold leaf mounted on paper is cut into narrow strips, then wound round a central core of orange silk. It gives a beautiful thread that is couched on top of the background fabric. Skill is needed to keep it twisted, and at the correct tension to prevent the orange core showing between the twisted gold strips. This particular thread was introduced to England and America in the mid nineteenth century and became impossible to buy from the 1970s onwards. Many embroiderers still retain their own stock, so it can be found appearing on present-day pieces of work. Its colour can vary from deep orange and red golds to the very pale greeny golds, and has a much richer hue than the jap gold substitutes that are available today. Prior to the availability of jap gold in

52 Detail of letter case or kincob, presented to Queen Victoria on one of her Jubilees, 1887–1897. Looped purl forms the petals of formalized flowers. Indian. (*Osborne House, Isle of Wight.*

Reproduced by gracious permission of Her Majesty the Queen)

thc nineteenth century there were similar threads from different sources. See *Aurum battutum, Cyprus gold, Venice gold.*

JAP SILVER

Made by the same method as jap gold, but using silver round a grey silk core. See *Jap gold.*

JAP GOLD AND SILVER SUBSTITUTE

A thread made in a similar manner to the original jap gold, but using a plated alloy instead of the gold leaf. It is handled in exactly the same manner, but is easier to use, as it does not come unwound so easily. (*See Fig. 51.*)

JEWELS

See *Stones.*

KID (Gloving kid)

Very fine leather that is easy to sew and manipulate. Kid is available with finishes in different shades of gold, silver and platinum. See *Leather.*

KINCOB

An Indian term for a brocade of gold or silver or both. It became a name for the richly embroidered metal thread covers, cases, envelopes or containers which encased the addresses sent to Queen Victoria by the Indian Princes on the occasions of her two Jubilees.

KINKHAB

Obviously connected to 'kincob', the name given to the very heavy metal thread embroidery worked on velvet or satin from Lucknow. It was made for articles and clothes used by the native courts on state occasions. With the integration of the states in the Indian Union, the demand has almost died out and the *kinkhab* worker is trying his hand at lighter embroidery to meet the demands of the market.

KNITTING YARNS

There is a wide selection available of gold, silver, bronze, copper and other metallic-coloured knitting ribbons and yarns that can be incorporated into metal thread embroidery, both hand

53a Processional cross which adapts to a free-standing altar cross. For St Anne's Church, Highgate, London. (*Jean Panter*)

and machine. Because they nearly all have a strong lurex finish they need to be used selectively and with subtlety to give the most rewarding results.

LAMA

The very thin gilded or plated metal sheet from which fine strips, similar to plate, or decorative motifs, may be cut or punched. Both are a popular addition to Indian embroidery.

LAMINAE (Paillons, Spangles)

Small flat or raised shapes cut from lama, used to enrich textiles throughout the ages in societies where precious metals were worked.

LAMÉ

A fabric woven from metallic thread, taking its name from lama. Because of its textural quality it can give very good effects in small areas as a contrast to metallic leathers or areas of metal thread.

LEATHER

Today the tanned skins of animals

may be obtained in a wide selection of weights, finishes, and colours. The metallic finished leathers, incorporated with metal thread embroidery, are of immense value. Care needs to be taken that leather is not used in too large an unbroken area, as the flat shine can lack quality and interest of design. In most cases, it is improved by padding it to give a contoured effect. Many leathers are supple enough to manipulate, quilt, or wrap around cords, etc. These techniques all add extra dimensions to the work. Soft leathers of various finishes can be used for articles of dress, and provide an attractive background for areas of metal thread embroidery. See *TECHNIQUES: Leather.*

LINEN

Linen fabrics are made from processed flax. Linen yarns are very

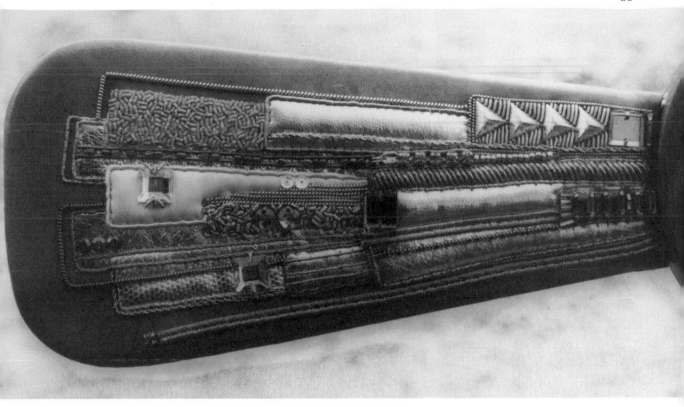

53b Detail of 53a.

LUREX

The trademark of the manufacturers, which has now become the generic term given to metal-coated plastic yarns. These are not true metal yarns, but yarns made of metallized plastic. For certain uses a fine monofilament nylon thread is added for strength. A wide selection of different weights of fabric and thread, suitable for all purposes, is now available.

MACHINE EMBROIDERY THREAD

Available in a comprehensive range of colours and shades and in different weights, 100% cotton and fast-dyed. There is an excellent range in 100% viscose rayon which has a silk-like lustre. There are metallized threads in

good colours including a range of golds, silver and copper. They vary from manufacturer to manufacturer as to colours, tone of gold, and amount of shine, so it is worth checking the market carefully.

MALTESE SILK
See *Horsetail silk*.

MEMBRANE GOLD
See *Cyprus Gold*.

METAL THREADS

Both traditional metal threads and those developed by modern technology are available for the embroiderer. There is check (silver and gold); imitation jap in copper, gold and silver; jap gold and silver substitute; knitting yarns; lurex; machine embroidery threads of various types; passing threads in copper, gold and silver; pearl purls and purl in copper, gold and silver; plate in gold and silver; tambour in copper, gold and silver; aluminium, copper, gold and silver twists; and some fine wires in

copper, gold, silver and several colours.

METALLIC BEADS
See *Beads*.

METALLIC-COLOURED YARNS

With the achievements of technology and the dictates of fashion, the embroiderer has a wide choice of metallic yarns. It is not necessary for a thread to be able to pass easily through the fabric; it can be couched, knitted or woven into position, so incorporating it into the design. Thus any yarn whose colour and texture appeals can be used.

MICA (Mirror glass, shisha)

A shiny, almost transparent mineral that was used in small pieces to add glitter to Tudor and Stuart embroidery. It may be seen in some stumpwork pieces. It was used on Indian and eastern embroideries until it was replaced by shisha (mirror glass) in the twentieth century. See *Mirror glass*.

strong, have a beautiful quality and do not rot. They are woven into a wide selection of fabrics of all weights. See *Background fabric* and *Backing fabric*.

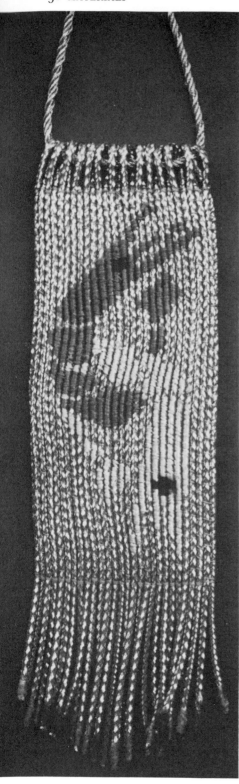

54 Purse. Laid lurex cord with *or nué* prawn. (*Diana Dolman, London College of Fashion*)

55 Set of robe ornaments, decorated with couched and coiled gilt thread. The daisy-type flower has shisha glass as its centre. India. (*Embroiderers' Guild Collection*)

MIRROR GLASS (Shisha glass, mica)

Used in small pieces, incorporated with embroidery, to make richly decorated textiles. The reflective surface has a soft blue tinge which gives a marvellous contrast to the very strong colours that are combined with it in Indian and Pakistani embroidery. See *TECHNIQUES: Shisha*.

MOIRE

A French term describing a finishing process which gives a watery appearance on the surface of a fabric. The best results are seen on silk fabrics, though the effect can also be achieved on cotton or manmade fibres. See *Background fabric*.

MOULD

In embroidery a mould can refer to: (1) the wooden foundation which forms the heads of a tassel over which knotted buttonhole stitch or other finishes may be worked; (2) the base formed from wood, cotton wool or waste pieces, which gives shape to the hands, heads and other areas in seventeenth-century stumpwork.

MUSLIN

First woven in Mosul, Iraq, near the Turkish border, this was the name given to a variety of plain woven cotton fabrics. In India, it is the term that has described a fine, soft cotton cloth for at least three hundred years, and that is how it is recognized in Britain. In the United States, the term 'muslin' covers a far wider selection of cotton clothes. See *Background fabric*.

NAP

Pile of a fabric; most strongly appreciated on velvet. The light falling on the nap one way makes the fabric look dark; if the fabric is turned by 180°, the fabric looks light, depending on whether the nap is lying upwards (against the light) or downwards (with the light). Great care needs to be taken to check background fabrics, applied pieces, ribbons etc. for the direction of the nap, so that the required effect is obtained.

56 White muslin dress embroidered with silver, *c.* 1780. (*Museum of London*)

NET

A very open mesh fabric produced by hand or machine, in which the threads are twisted or knotted to keep them in position. See *Background fabric.*

NOIL

See *Bourette.*

NON-WOVEN FABRICS

See *Felt* and *Handmade paper.*

NUN'S VEILING

A lightweight, soft, good-quality worsted cloth made in a plain weave. See *Background fabric.*

OES (Owes)

Small metal eyelets with a central hole, which were grouped to form a trimming on articles of dress in the late sixteenth and early seventeenth centuries.

OMBRE

Shaded – can apply to threads which are space dyed in one colour, so that they are shaded along their length from light to dark, and to light again in regular intervals.

ORGANDIE

A thin lightweight fabric woven from fine, tightly twisted cotton yarns. It is transparent and has a permanently crisp finish. Combined with metal thread techniques, organdie laid over one, or several layers of fabric, can build up to an interesting background. See *Background fabric.*

ORGANZA

A pure silk fabric which is similar to organdie in production. It can be obtained in the most beautiful colours, many of which are shot. This effect is created by using different coloured yarns in the weft to those used in the warp, and because the yarns are shiny a luminous or iridescent effect can be produced. See *Background fabric.*

OWES

See *Oes.*

57 Two sizes of passing thread, 6s and 4s.

58 Pearl purls.

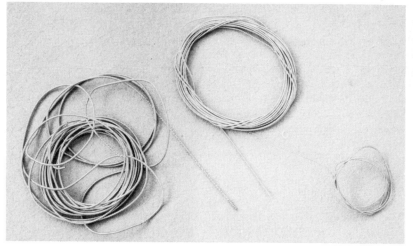

PAILLETTES

See *Sequin.*

PAILLONS

See *Sequin.*

PASSEMENT (Passemayne)

A term which covers all types of trimmings, including lace, which incorporates metal threads or jet.

PASSING

A fine flexible metal thread with a silk, nylon or cotton core, which can be sewn through the fabric. Although it is easy to handle, it is advisable to use a needle with quite a large eye, and only short lengths of thread, to help prevent the passing thread wearing and fraying in the working. It was used by the Elizabethans for plaited braid stitch, chain stitch outlines, buttonhole fillings, and for work on canvas or fine linen combined with silk or wools. It is one of the less shiny metal threads because it has a very slightly textured surface, so it can provide a smooth quieter area where the eye can rest, making a contrast to the rich texture of cords, and the moving gleam of jap gold substitute. Passing can be obtained in aluminium, copper, gold and silver, and in various synthetic substitutes.

PEARL PURL

A hollow spiral of wire like a tightly wound spring. It can be pulled out to show up the spiral as a strong texture, or couched down as it is. But it is only

59 Mule (one of a pair), pearl and metal thread embroidery on velvet. Indian. (*Osborne House, Isle of Wight. Reproduced by gracious permission of Her Majesty the Queen*)

when it is pulled out, however slightly, that it becomes rigid and easily controlled. It is obtainable in four sizes in copper, gold and silver. See *Purls*.

PEARLS

Pearls and seed pearls have been combined with embroidery from the earliest days. They were sometimes mounted in metal, like other jewels, before being sewn into place, but more usually they were pierced and sewn on like beads. Pearls, or their former position, can be seen on the Butler Bowden Cope, made in the early fourteenth century during the period of Opus Anglicanum. Elizabethan portraits show the popularity of pearls for decorating the elaborate court dresses. Baroque pearls with their soft pinks, greens and greys have also been popular with embroiderers at various periods. Pearls can still combine very

happily with metal thread embroidery in the right situation. See *Artificial pearls*.

PINS

An essential part of every embroiderer's equipment. It is well worth the expense of having good ones, which will neither mark the fabric through rust, nor make over-large holes. If the points are blunt, they break the threads of the background instead of passing between the woven threads. The fine steel pins with coloured glass heads are useful for mounting and making-up jobs, but for normal use the long fine steel pins are excellent.

PIPING CORD

Available in a variety of thicknesses, piping cord can be covered with leather to give a strong line. It can form a base for basketwork filling so long as it is a hard cord, and is well twisted as it is sewn in position. This is because some piping cords seem to be quite soft, and without the smooth round finish which is required when forming a foundation for metal thread patterns. (*See Fig. 88.*)

PLATE

A thin flat strip of metal that may be couched down as it is, or crimped or folded to break up its very harsh reflecting light. In historical pieces, especially from Persia and Turkey, plate can be seen to have been regularly worked through the background fabric, but that is rare in Britain. It was regularly used for rich ornamentation on dress in the eighteenth century, and on military uniforms. See *TECHNIQUES*.

POLYTHENE BAGS

Although plastic bags are excellent for transporting embroidery as protection against dirt and weather, embroidery should never be stored in plastic, as changes in climatic condition can cause condensation which in turn causes discoloration of some of the metal threads, deterioration of the fabrics and distortion of the yarns.

POUND BEADS
See *Beads*.

PURLS (Bullion)
Fine wire coiled into a hollow spring.

OPPOSITE

60 Detail of chasuble embroidered in silver thread, plate, and paillettes on crimson silk. Italian, late eighteenth century. Note plate in centre of petals of main flower. (*Embroiderers' Guild Collection*)

OPPOSITE BELOW

61 Turkish wedding veil using plate. Anatolia, nineteenth century. (*Embroiderers' Guild Collection*)

RIGHT

62 Assorted purls.

BELOW RIGHT

63 Detail from a sampler, showing purl with bright bullion No. 5, 'Caterpillar'. (*Jean Panter*)

They are made in many types to give different qualities of texture and brilliance, and each type in up to nine sizes. The number of sizes made varies with the manufacturer, as does the quality. The modern purls do not tarnish as badly as those made in previous years, due to a smaller percentage of precious metal being used in their manufacture. They are very pliable and springy, and are cut into short lengths to be sewn down like a bead. See *TECHNIQUES*.

Bright or smooth purl A highly polished round coil with a strong reflection.

Rough purl Has the same round section as the smooth, but is much duller to give a contrast.

Bright check Made by winding the wire on to a square mould, so that the angled wire sparkles with different lights.

Check purl Made in the same way as bright check, but the reflecting areas are smaller so that it has a duller appearance.

Grit The name sometimes given to the minute off-cuts of lengths of purl, which can be used for texturing or seeding an area. See *Frize* and *Badla*.

Purls Available in copper, gold and silver.

Pearl purl A hollow spiral of wire like

a tightly wound spring, and much stiffer than the purls. It can be pulled out to show up the spiral as a strong texture, or couched down as it is. Once it is extended it loses its spring and gains stability, so is very easy to couch on to the required line. It is obtainable in four sizes in copper, gold and silver.

PURSE SILK (Netting silk)

Purse silk was a round, even silk thread with a firm twist so that it did not fluff up with wear. Mainly used for crocheting purses in the nineteenth century, but was also used for ecclesiastical embroidery.

ROCAILLES

See *Beads*.

ROCOCO

A metal thread which is similar to a crinkle, but with a slightly longer undulation to it.

ROUGH PURL

See *Purls*.

RUSSIA BRAID (Soutache)

A narrow braid made of two cords which have been united by plaited metal threads.

SATIN

The name of a type of weave. The fabric, which is traditionally made of silk, has a smooth, unbroken surface texture. There are many types of satin fabrics, some still made in silk, others in cotton or a variety of synthetic fibres. See *Background fabric*.

SCRIM

A thin, loosely woven linen cloth made for household cleaning purposes. Its quality has attracted the embroiderer for many years, and is used for a variety of pulled work techniques, both hand and machine. It combines very well with metal threads so long as it is mounted on a backing fabric to show through the loosely woven fibres and to give it added strength to carry the weight of the embroidery. See *Background fabric*.

64a Red wool facecloth jacket embroidered with gold purl, using laid and couched work over padding. Greece, 1860–80. (*Embroiderers' Guild Collection*)

64b Detail of 64a.

SEQUIN

A mid nineteenth-century term which replaced 'paillette'.

Paillette Previously used to describe a thin flat disc used on textiles for ornamentation, in groups or in conjunction with embroidery. 'Paillette' is still used as the trade name for a sequin, and covers the flat punched-out shapes, usually circular; but they can be oval, heart-shaped, flower-shaped, or anything else that the manufacturer likes to produce. The hole or holes may be in any position appropriate to the shape. When 'paillette' was the term in everyday use, it normally had an adjective in front to describe its shape. In the eighteenth century mentions of paillettes referred to small rings of gold flattened with a planishing hammer.

Couvette (Teste) The name for the slightly concave paillettes, usually very small, that can be found on many historical pieces.

Spangles Small flat circular decorations cut out from very fine sheets of brass, copper, gold or silver. Originally they were made from flattened loops of wire. See *Laminae* and *Oes*.

Paillons An eighteenth-century coloured spangle cut out from thin sheets of silver and varnished in different colours.

SEQUIN WASTE

The strip of cellulose or plastic from which modern sequin discs are punched, leaving a design of regular holes. The waste product can be cut up and rearranged to form more interesting irregular shapes, and purls or stitching then applied on top to give a textured area.

SEWING THREAD

A thread especially made for the application of metal threads, braids and cords was Maltese thread, but this is now no longer manufactured. Some synthetic sewing threads in old-gold colours are quite pleasant to use, and invisible nylon thread, although its length of life has not yet been proven.

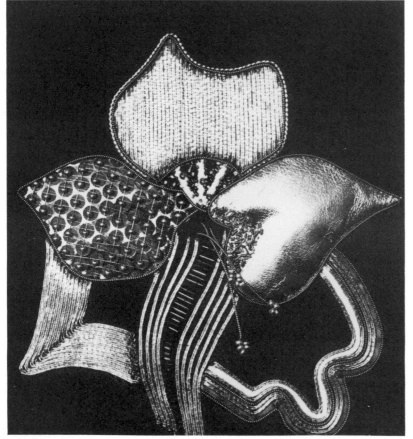

65 Silk fan embroidered with silk flowers, spangles, and gold thread in a stitched 'fringe' to echo the semicircular shapes. Mounted on tortoiseshell sticks. (*Schrieber fan reproduced by courtesy of the Trustees of the British Museum*)

66 'Amaryllis', showing use of sequin waste. (*Ruth A. Morrison*)

There are new, thicker rayon machine embroidery threads in a range of colours which are well worth experimenting with, but silk sewing threads are still the preference of many embroiderers. One strand of stranded cotton, well waxed, is also suitable.

SHADED THREADS
See *Ombré*.

SHANTUNG
A rough, plain weave silk fabric woven from uneven yarns, which gives a textured effect. See *Background fabric*.

SHISHA GLASS (Mica)
See *Mirror glass*.

1 'Fuchsia'. *(Mary Tasker)*.

2 'Tam o'shantas'. *(Mary Tasker)*.

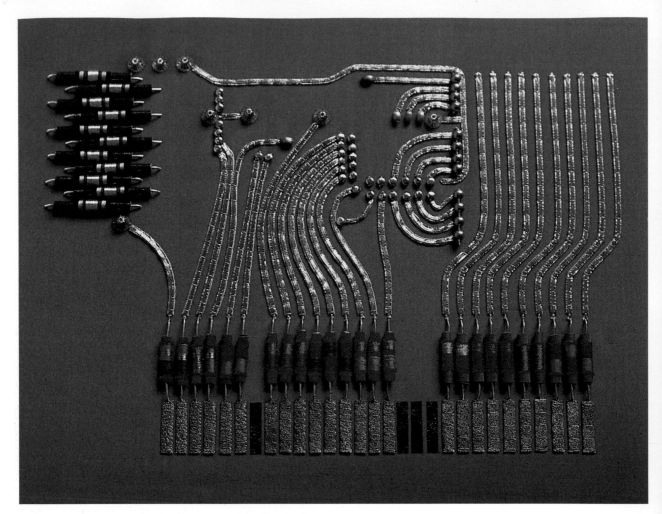

3 'Hi-Tech'. The design is based on the lines and forms found in
   printed circuits. To accentuate the metallic lines, narrow strips
   of silver leather were couched down in place, then silver
   threads couched on top. Sequins, beads and purl were used
   with tiny handmade tubes of leather and silk to indicate the
   details on the circuits. 30 x 40 cm (12 x 16 in.) approx.
   (Hannah Frew Paterson).

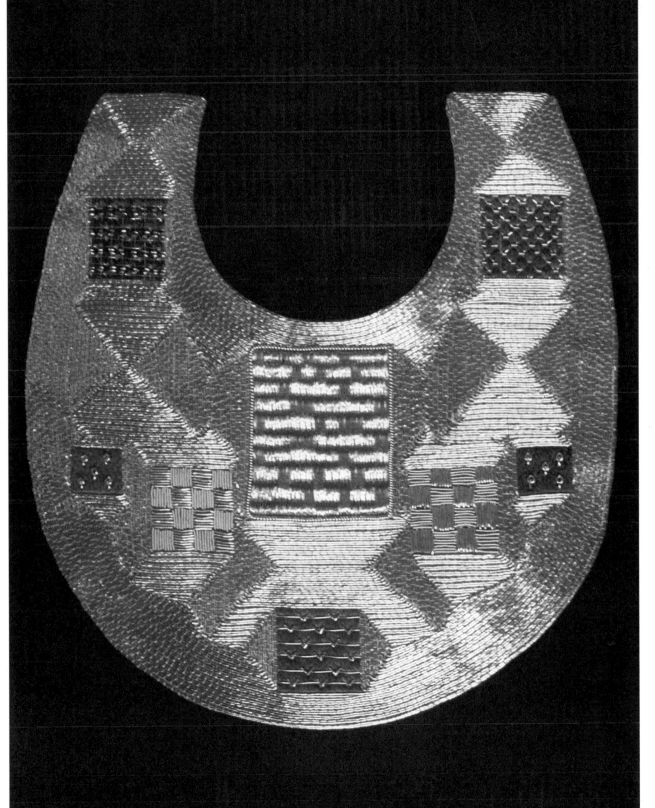

5   'The Last Rose of Summer'. *(Ann Sutton)*.

6 The cross from the Festal frontal, suggesting water. The work is highly raised. *(Designed by Jane Lemon and worked by Mollie Collins, the Sarum Group. By kind permission of the Dean and Chapter of Salisbury Cathedral).*

8   The Head of Christ, worked in *or nué*. *(Beryl Dean MBE 1983-4).*

7   **Opposite** Chalice, worked in *or nué* with leather, and highly
     padded. A detail from the Energy frontal. *(Designed by Jane
     Lemon and worked by Mollie Collins, the Sarum Group. By kind
     permission of the Dean and Chapter of Salisbury Cathedral).*

9 Neckpiece. Machine lace and stainless steel structures.
   (Alison Shreeve).

10 Detail of swimming terrapins on woman's formal robe
    (Furisode), from Japan. Blue satin with a ground of applied
    gold leaf, embroidered with twisted and floss silks and with
    gilt paper thread wound around a silk core. Laid and couched
    work, partly over padding, with long-and-short, straight and
    satin stitches and knots. This combination of applied gold leaf
    with embroidery was a Japanese technique known as *Nuihaku*.
    (Embroiderers' Guild Collection).

SILK FABRIC

Silk fabric has a marvellous sheen and lively appearance. There are more than forty types of fabric made from silk, and they vary in weight and effect, some being fine and soft, whilst others are stiff and formal. The textured dupion silk woven from uneven yarn is one that many embroiderers find combines well with the metal threads, each setting off the other to best advantage. See *Background fabric*.

SILK THREAD

Made from the continuous filament produced by the silkworm, it comes in a great variety of types and weight. It varies from a very fine sewing thread to a heavily textured knitting yarn. At the end of the 1980s a Japanese thread, and an Italian twisted silk are available for embroidery.

SILVER GILT THREAD

Pure gold thread may be found on the tenth-century Durham stole, but after that all the thread, including that found on the magnificent Opus Anglicanum embroidery, was silver gilt. This is a fine strip of silver, which is then gilded. Sometimes the metal was wound over a silk core, at other times drawn into a pliable wire thread. It is impossible to tell how the threads were made merely from looking at early pieces of embroidery.

SILVER THREADS

Available in the same types as those in gold. See *Gold threads*.

SIPERS GOLD

See *Cyprus gold*.

SKANNY

A silk and gold twisted thread produced in Russia in the fifteenth and sixteenth centuries.

SKIN GOLD

See *Cyprus gold*.

SMOOTH PURL

See *Purl*.

SOUTACHE

See *Russia braid*.

SPANGLES

See *Sequin*.

SPRAY FABRIC PROTECTOR

There are several of these on the mar-

67 Silk apron, embroidered with coloured silk and metal threads. English, early eighteenth century. (*By courtesy of the Trustees of the Victoria & Albert Museum*)

ket for the prevention of tarnish and for protection from the absorption of dust. It is advisable to test the selected one on a spare piece of fabric and samples of the threads used, before spraying the actual embroidery, to make absolutely certain that it doesn't have an adverse effect.

STAMPS

The manufactured shaped moulds used for the padded foundations of raised metal thread work on regalia.

STONES (Gems, Jewels)

Precious and semi-precious stones Have been used in conjunction with metal thread embroidery in ceremonial use for both Church and State, to show wealth and status, from the earliest times.

Imitation stones Stones of glass and plastic have made similar richness of design available for the fashion world, and the general embroiderer.

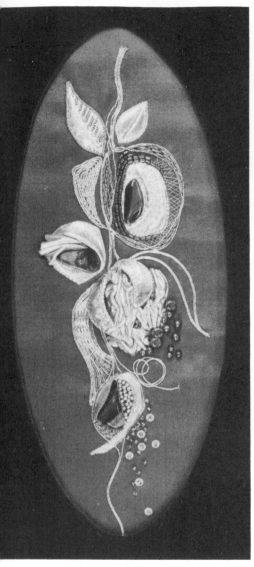

68a 'Autumn'. With tiger's eye stones, beads, leather and metal threads. (*Connie Pepper*)

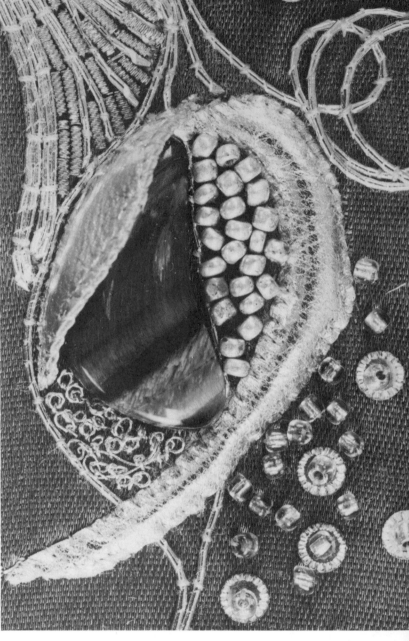

68b Detail.

STRANDED COTTONS

Available from several manufacturers, and are colourfast. They are made in a six-stranded thread so that as many strands as required can be used for stitching, couching and tying down couched threads.

STRING

String of different thicknesses is used for padding and fillings. When being used to raise metal threads, it is advisable to dye it with a waterproof ink to match the thread. The string needs to be smooth and tightly twisted.

TAFFETA

The term 'taffeta' comes from the Persian word *tafta*, meaning a glossy twist. Taffeta is usually made from a high-twist silk or synthetic fibre yarn, giving it the crisp paper-like quality for which it is known. In medieval Europe the term 'taffeta' was used to describe a variety of lightweight silk fabrics. In the seventeenth century the terms 'taffatie' and 'taffety' were being used in Bengal, where silk fabrics similar to those woven in Persia were made and exported to Europe. Within the term taffeta there is still a variation of weight, quality and finishes. See *Background fabric*.

TAMBOUR THREAD (Filé thread)

A silver gilt or a synthetic thread, a little finer than passing thread, which can be used in a needle. It can be found in copper, silver and gold.

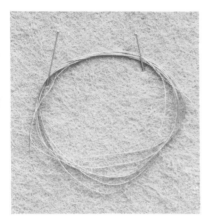

69 Tambour thread.

70 Detail of one of a pair of garlands presented by Her Highness Banaras to Queen Victoria. Gold purl laid on the animals, edged with pearl purl; laid sequin background with tinsel fringe and tassels. (*Sandringham House Museum. Reproduced by gracious permission of Her Majesty the Queen*)

Because it was originally made for working with a tambour hook, it is usually softer than a passing thread.

THREAD FOR SEWING DOWN METAL THREADS

See *Sewing threads*.

TINSEL

A flattened copper wire of various widths which has been given a gold, silver or other coloured metallic finish. It has always referred generally to any fabric trimming that has a high degree of glitter.

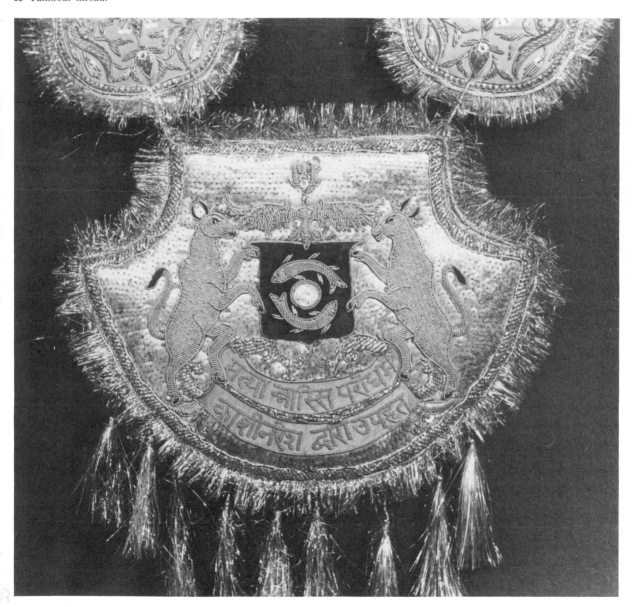

71 Minature deckchair, 20 cm (8 in.) in height. The seat has a top panel of machine embroidery in gold and coloured threads, worked on vanishing muslin, and an underpanel of machine-quilted cream silk. (*Dorothy Walker, 1982. Embroiderers' Guild Collection*)

TISSUE PAPER
See *Acid-free tissue paper*.

TOSCAS
See *Beads*.

TRACING PAPER
The transparent paper used in the transferring of designs to fabric. See also *Greaseproof paper*.

TWISTS
Metal threads made up of two or more strands twisted firmly together. There is a fine one which may be sewn with, but the range of heavier ones are couched into position. There are also some heavy plaited cords, in several sizes, which the manufacturers call 'twist'. (*See Figs 40, 41 and 42.*)

VANISHING MUSLIN
This relatively new fabric may be embroidered over by hand or machine, making sure that there is sufficient stitchery to hold the motifs together. The muslin can then be melted away by ironing with a hot iron, leaving a lace-like effect. Make sure that the threads used will withstand the heat of the iron, and will not dissolve at the same time. See *TECHNIQUES: Water-soluble fabrics*.

VELVET
A warp-cut, pile fabric, originally made with a silk pile and cotton back. Different types of velvet vary enormously in thickness and length of pile, and in quality to the touch. Because of the pile, special considerations need to be made when velvet is used as a background. See *Background fabric*, and *TECHNIQUES: Velvet techniques*.

VELLUM
Very thin sheets of calfskin which was first dyed yellow with saffron to blend with the gold thread, then marked with a design and cut in bulk with a cutting iron to be used as padding under gold. See *Cartisane*.

VENICE GOLD
Venice gold superseded the earlier Cyprus gold thread. It was imported into England from Venice in the sixteenth and seventeenth centuries.

VILENE
A non-woven interlining, which may be obtained in several weights from very fine up to a heavy pelmet Vilene. Also available as an iron-on bonding interlining which makes a soft fabric easier to control. Vilene has no grain, so does not stretch.

VIYELLA
Proprietary brand name for a light weight twill-woven cloth made from 55% wool and 45% cotton. See *Background fabric*.

WADDING
The soft filling used in quilting. Traditionally this was either carded wool or cotton. Synthetic waddings are now available, including polyester wadding in several thicknesses. In metal thread work, wadding is only occasionally needed where some quilting is being incorporated, or a softer effect than padding with felt is required.

WATER-SOLUBLE FABRICS
There are now two fabrics on the market which dissolve when placed in water; one is for use with boiling water, and the other with cold. Both are much easier to use than the original vanishing muslin. Hand or machine embroidery can be worked on the fabric, care being taken to ensure that there is sufficient linking stitchery to hold the piece together once the background is dissolved by dipping in water. See *TECHNIQUES: Water-soluble fabrics*.

WEBBING
A narrow woven band of hemp, used on the two rollers of a slate frame. One long edge of the webbing is nailed to the wooden roller of the frame; the other long edge is oversewn to the folded edge of the backing fabric which will carry the embroidery. It is important that these two lengths of webbing are carefully unpicked from the backing fabric when the embroidery is complete, otherwise if it is cut or deteriorates it makes mounting up for the next piece very difficult, and the webbing may have to be replaced.

WIRES
The name sometimes given to the group of purls and pearl purls.

YELLOW RAISING THREAD
A special yarn made for working satin stitch padding under small areas of gold work.

TECHNIQUES

ANGLES (to turn metal threads)
See *Couching*.

APPLIQUE (Applied work)
The laying of a required shape of fabric on the background to add variation of texture, colour or tone. In order to make the applied piece lie flat and not wrinkle, it is essential that its straight grain should lie exactly on the straight grain of the background. If the design demands that the straight grain of the small shape runs through the centre of the shape, and so lies off the straight grain of the background, any later problems can be avoided by applying the small shape to a fine iron-on Vilene before applying it to the background. If the fabric is thin, soft, or in any way difficult to handle, it is well worth while applying it to a bonding agent, then ironing it on to the background to secure it in place whilst it is being sewn down by hand or machine.

72a Cope. A design to display a free but disciplined use of gold work techniques, with silk floss embroidery and silk

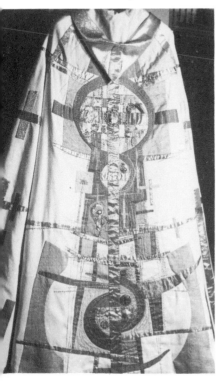

appliqué on white. Detail shows use of gold couching, purls, and padding of string or felt. Curved lines display the shine of the thread. The design aims to have a spiritual feeling of space and is influenced by the emphasis on space exploration at the time. (*Barbara Dawson, 1966. Chelmsford Cathedral*)

72b Detail.

73a Straight grain of the motif lying on the straight grain of the background. **b** The leaf motif should be applied to a fine iron-on Vilene before being placed on the background.

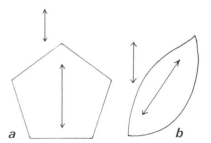

Methods of sewing the shape to be applied into position (a) Zig-zag stitch on the machine; (b) a zig-zag stitch by hand; (c) by turning under a narrow hem and securing to the background with ladder stitch. It is easier to achieve a

74 'Flowerpot' embroidered cushion cover. Designed by William Morris and embroidered by his daughter May Morris, c. 1880. (*The William Morris Gallery, Walthamstow, London*)

sharp line on the edge if the fabric is turned over a Vilene backing. This can vary in weight according to the size of the applied piece and the type of fabric used. Using Vilene also avoids any problems of the line of the turning showing through to the right side, as a line or a shadow; (d) It was traditional before the 1950s to use satin, blanket, or buttonhole stitch over the raw edge, but these give a strong heavy line which is often not

desired in the present day work; (e) Having sewn the applied shape to the background with a zig-zag or overcast stitch to prevent the edges from fraying, a thread, threads, cord or braid of any type can be couched over the edge to conceal the stitching, and to give a decorative finish. This makes a strong contribution to the design of the whole piece, and care must be taken to consider whether the edge should be left with a tidy machine-stitch finish, a

75 Screen panel embroidered with silk and gold on satin. Miss E. D. Bradby, 1899. (*By courtesy of the Trustees of the Victoria & Albert Museum*)

self-coloured couched line, or built up with a decorative line that may vary in weight, tone or colour on different sections of the appliqué. It is not necessary to continue the same treatment round the whole edge of the applied shape. See *Ladder stitch* and *Motif*; *MATERIALS: Bonding* and *Vilene*.

ARABESQUE STYLE

Widely used for embroidery in the sixteenth century. Its curving lines and scrolls were derived from Islamic art. The term can also refer to the intricate surface decoration, very often based on complex geometric patterns, which again originated in Islamic design.

ARCADED

A design where figures, buildings, or any other subject are framed by embroidered arches. This may be seen in many of the ecclesiastical pieces throughout the centuries from Opus Anglicanum onwards in England and Europe. It reflects the style used by the popular painters of religious art. It is in the last phase of Opus Anglicanum (1300–1350) that the basic design of the copes has a framework of arcading radiating from the centre to link the individual motifs.

Foliation Tracery formed by an arrangement of foils (or small arcs) which are separated by cusps (the points where the foils meet), in Gothic architecture, e.g. cinquefoil, quatrefoil, trefoil.

Foliated arcading Usually, with twists in the columns which sprout leaves. The columns on the Butler Bowden Cope have four twists and sprout oak leaves with acorns.

Crockets Crockets often decorate the upper side of the more ornate arches. The Butler Bowden Cope has three of

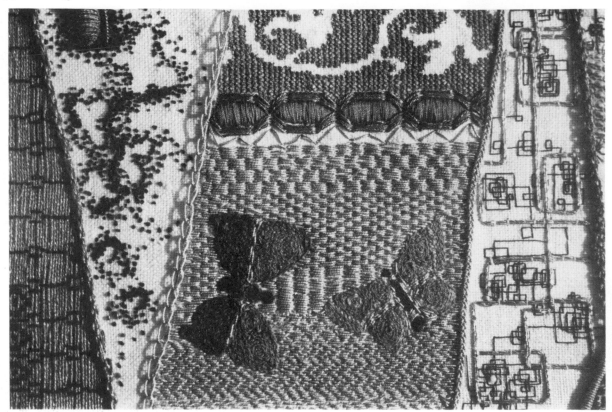

76 Gold work sampler (detail). (*Suellen Pedley*)

these decorative 'mouldings' on each arch.

ART DECO
The name given to the highly stylized angular designs, using unnatural colours with an intense interest in texture, belonging to the 1920s and 30s.

ART NEEDLEWORK
The late nineteenth-century revolt against the prevailing style of embroidery. Art needlework stressed line and colour, and the interpretation of the design by the individual. (*See Fig. 74.*)

ART NOUVEAU
A reaction in Europe and America against the high decoration of Victorian crafts. The movement was seen in strength between 1890 and 1910. John Ruskin and William Morris were two of the first to emphasize the importance of line in design, with decorative details taking a subordinate place. A strong embroidery department at the Glasgow School of Art, under the influence of Francis and Jessie Newbery, and later Ann Macbeth and Charles Rennie Macintosh, was influential in the teaching of good design.

ASSISI EMBROIDERY
A cross stitch technique, where the background is worked in cross stitch, the pattern is left plain (voided), and Holbein stitch is used to outline the design. With modern metallic threads this can certainly be adapted to gold work, and may even spark off ideas for working elaborate gold backgrounds to set off motifs, similar to the beautiful gold laid work backgrounds of nine of the remaining Opus Anglicanum copes.

ASYMMETRY
Where the exact corresponding parts on either side of the central line are not mirror images, nor necessarily have equal weight or proportion. The resulting whole, however, has an overall pleasing balance and movement of line which is of more interest to the beholder than a symmetrical piece, where both halves are identical.

AURIPHRYGIUM
The term given by the Romans to Phrygian work (Opus Phrygium), which was work embroidered in gold alone. The Phrygians were important traders of Asiatic and Babylonian embroideries, which they shipped to Greece and Italy. In time, 'auriphrygium' came to apply to all embroidery that used any gold in its composition; hence the English medieval term of 'orphrey' for the bands of embroidery used to decorate ecclesiastical furnishings or vestments.

BALANCE MARKS (Reference marks)
Where areas of embroidery are to be worked separately and assembled at a later date (or two pieces of fabric are to be seamed together), it is very much

easier, quicker and more accurate for tacking marks to be sewn on to the background and the pieces to be applied (or the two lengths of fabric), to show their relative positions. This should be done at the earliest possible stage when designs are being traced out, or work is being planned.

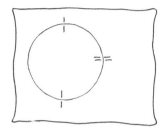

77 Balance marks.

BALL BUTTONS

Decorative buttons may be made by covering a round wooden bead or mould with buttonhole stitch, ball stitch or knotted buttonhole stitch, worked with a metal twist, passing

78 Turk's head knot. Using a thick, firm, wiry thread, make the preliminary loops, leaving them the size of the required finished ball. Continue to weave the needle in and out following the thread as shown by the dotted line, until three rows have been completed lying side by side. Mould the ball into shape as the weaving is worked.

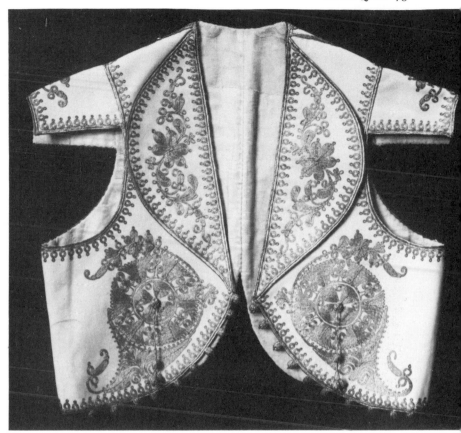

79a Light grey facecloth jacket with couched gilt thread and braid. Plaited gilt thread buttons decorate the front edge and form tassels. Turkish, nineteenth century. (*Embroiderers' Guild Collection*)

79b Detail.

thread, or metallic yarn. If a traditional thread is used, it should be waxed to make it more pliable. If a knotted stitch is to be used, then it is likely that the basic colour of the bead will show through between the stitches, so the bead should either be first covered with a fine silk, or dyed to a suitable colour. It must be noted that these buttons are for decoration and that the metal threads will not stand up to the continual wear and tear of being pushed in and out of buttonholes. See *Tassels* (Ball stitch).

BARS

See *Composite stitches*.

BARBED QUATREFOIL

See *Quatrefoil*.

BARGELLO WORK

See *Florentine stitch*.

BAROQUE

The name given to the extravagant and florid European style of *c.* 1630–1710.

BASKET STITCH FILLING

Worked by laying threads over a foundation of parallel lengths of string sewn down at fixed intervals. The undulations formed by sewing down a rich metallic thread (jap gold was often used) imitate the various weaves found on basketware, and the changing fall of light gives a very rich textural quality.

The couching thread which ties down the metal thread may be in self colour, or the shadows accentuated by using a darker-toned colour. This helps to throw up the pattern. The thread needs to be strong and to be waxed. *The string* chosen for the foundation needs to be of a thickness that is in proportion to the area being filled, and to the size of the finished piece, otherwise it can be too strong and heavy and throws the other areas out of balance. See *Padding*. Different weights of string may be used together in the same area to give varied patterns, or a graduated padding. *The metal thread* is usually laid in pairs, but

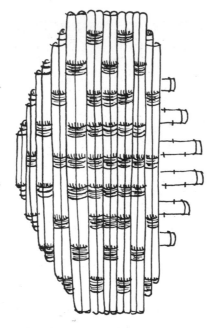

80 Basket stitch filling. Pairs of metal threads, or a single thicker flat braid, are carried over two rows of string, then couched down. By alternating the couching positions, a pattern is built up. Varied patterns can be worked by changing the number of rows of string that the threads are carried over between couching stitches.

81 Basket stitch filling. (*Ann Sutton*)

BOTTOM
82 Detail from altar frontal showing basket stitch filling. (*Beryl Dean* MBE. *St Margaret's Church, King's Lynn*)

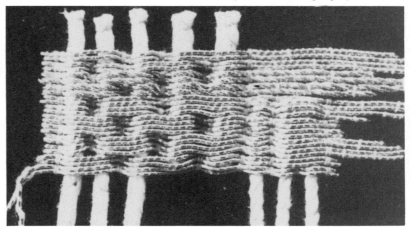

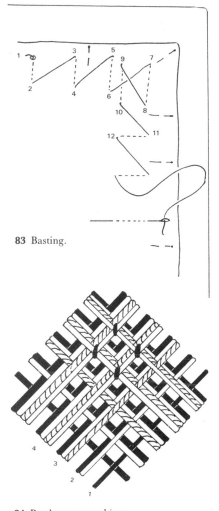

83 Basting.

84 Battlement couching.

it depends on the choice of thread and the effect required. Basket stitch filling may also be worked in pearl purl.

BASTING (Tacking)

Very often more control is required, and better tension maintained, than is possible with the normal enlarged running stitch associated with the term 'tacking'. The basting stitch which maintains a tension (as required when a piece of fabric is attached to the backing fabric on a frame), is worked by the thread on top of the fabric being carried forward, whilst the needle picks up the fabric in a stitch at right angles to the direction being worked. This gives a diagonal top stitch. See *Tacking*.

BATTLEMENT COUCHING

Originally a crewel work filling stitch, has been adapted and developed by Jennie Parry for canvas with metal threads and yarns. The original filling stitch is formed by a trellis of threads in four layers, each one being staggered by one thread of the ground fabric.

First trellis is prepared with the first parallel row of threads being laid with eight threads of linen between each

85a (*above*) **& b** (*overleaf*) Samplers using coloured and metal threads on canvas sprayed with car paint. Experiments with metal threads on canvas, many developed from battlement couching. (*Jennie Parry*)

row; then the second row of threads is laid at right angles, again leaving eight threads of linen between each row. *Second trellis* is laid with thread alongside the threads of the first row,

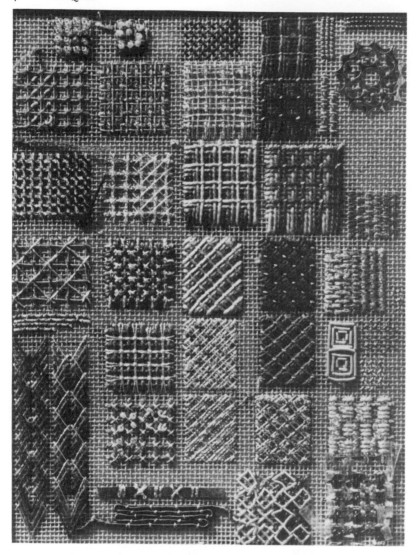

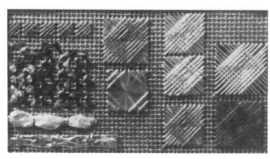

85b Detail of 85a.

86 Battlemented or crenellated profile.

using the holes of the linen to the right of the threads laid for the first trellis. The second trellis is completed with threads at right angles, laid in a similar manner. *Trellises three* and *four* are laid in a similar staggered manner. The fourth and last trellis is then tied down with a couching stitch at the intersection of its two rows.

BATTLEMENTED (crenellated)

Refers to the shapes formed by the battlements of a church or castle; hence the name given to the similar repetitive pattern that can be made for an edging, border, braided or embroidered band.

BATUZ WORK

Batuz work was mentioned in the inventories and royal wills from the eleventh to the fifteenth centuries. It referred to the low relief beaten gold plates representing animals, flowers, or heraldic devices which were incorporated in silk embroidery. Later it was known as 'bete' or 'beten work' and enriched metal thread embroidery of all types.

BEADING

When sewing on beads, it is advisable to wax the thread to give extra strength and to help prevent it from fraying when it rubs against the edges of the holes, which are often quite rough.

Attaching a single bead The thread is taken up through the fabric, through the hole of the bead, and down into the fabric; the stitch taken, is the length of the bead so that as little extra thread shows as possible. The bead is then lying on its side, with the hole parallel to the background. It is also advisable to work a couple of back stitches at regular intervals, on a spot where a bead will be placed, so that if a thread does break in the future all the beads will not drop off before it is possible to make a repair.

Attaching a single bead by using a bead The thread is taken up through the fabric, through the hole of the

87a Attaching a single bead with a back stitch. **b** A bead sewn on using a small bead. **c** A bead sewn on with a loop of purl. **d** Couching a string of beads. **e** Braid couched with beads.

88 Detail of a sampler, showing quilted leather over piping cord. (*D. M. Anderson*)

light. The density of the number of beads sewn on within an area depends entirely on the effect required. It is necessary to consider the effect of the weight of massed beads on the background fabric. Texturing may be achieved by couching strings of beads on in wavy lines to decorate an area, but a totally different effect is achieved. See *Tambour*.

Continuous line of beads Where beads need to be sewn on in a continuous line, they are threaded up first on to a strong thread, then couched between each bead, or group of beads, with a separate thread to hold them in position.

bead, then through a tiny bead (which needs to be larger than the hole in the original bead), down through the hole in the original bead and back through the fabric. The bead then stands with the hole at right angles to the background, with the tiny bead covering the hole and giving additional colour and texture.

Attaching a single bead by using a short length of purl The method is exactly the same as for attaching by using a bead. The cut purl can either be a tiny piece that lies like a bead, or it can be of a longer length. This will loop as the thread is returned through the bead, and gives a very decorative finish. Care needs to be taken that the loop of pearl is not too large for the bead, making it look unbalanced. If on the other hand an area is being filled with looped purl, this is a method of raising some of the loops, without having impractical long loops which may get caught, or are inclined to fall over if not tightly packed against other loops for support.

Texturing with beads This is normally achieved by sewing beads on singly, making sure that the beads lie at different angles to each other so as to emphasize the changing facets of

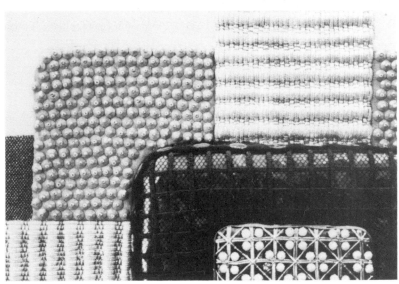

89 Beads sewn on with a smaller bead to make a heavily textured area. (*Beryl Dean MBE. St Margaret's Church, King's Lynn*)

Fringing A thread is sewn securely into whatever is to form the head of the fringe, then beads are strung as required for one strand of the fringe. A small bead is used as a 'stop' at the end of the strand, and the thread is re-threaded back the way that it has come to the head of the fringe, where it is backstitched. Each strand of the fringe is threaded in a similar manner, relating the pattern of beads from one strand to the next. Alternatively, coloured yarns or fine ribbons may be used to thread the beads on; these may then be knotted, wrapped, braided, or finished in tassels to give a richer fringe and to hold the beads in position.

Loops Loops may be made by bringing the thread through to the right side, stringing up a number of beads, then sewing the thread back through the fabric in the same place. Loops of equal or variable lengths can make decorative details, contribute to formal pattern, or be massed together as a textural area.

Decorative stitches Beads may be used singly or in groups, threaded on to the yarn at selected stages of working a decorative stitch to give added texture and/or colour.

Couching Couching may be worked with a bead or beads threaded on to the couching thread to tie down any lengths of yarn, cord, ribbon or strips of leather.

Raised shapes Raised shapes can be covered with beads. *When working over a metal or plastic ring*, tack it firmly into position then bring the needle up close to the outside of the ring. Thread on as many beads as are required to cover the edge of the ring to the inside, making sure that the thread goes straight over, and does not lie at an angle – unless this is required by the design. Take the needle through the background fabric and repeat the process. As the ring is covered it will be found that, since the inside of the ring is smaller than the outside, there is not always enough room to have a full length of beads, and the bare thread

needs to be carried down the inside of the ring. It depends on the size of the beads and the ring, as to what pattern fills the area best. It could be two full rows, then a half row of beads. It will be found that the half row is well supported by the next full row of beads, and so will stay firmly in place. *Rectangular or square shapes* can be cut from polystyrene. These should be tied down at regular intervals with coton perlé or another strong thread to form a base of bars on which to work a raised chain band or raised stem band. By threading small beads on to the working thread at each stage of the stitch, either a textured or a smooth surface can be created with the bead covering.

BETE (Beten)
See *Batuz work*.

BIAS CUT (Crossway, on the cross)
The term given to the crossway grain, the line drawn on the accurate 45° angle between the warp straight grain and the weft straight grain. This line has a natural stretch and therefore fabric cut on the cross may be used to mould round pipings, buttons, sculptures, and for manipulating without pleating. If the straight grain on the cut edge of a length of fabric is laid accurately on the selvedge of the fabric, the resulting fold will be the true cross grain, and bias lengths may be cut parallel to it.

90 Bias cut.

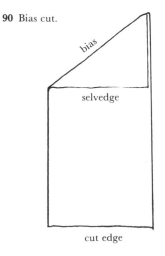

bias

selvedge

cut edge

BLACKWORK
This darning technique, first brought to Britain in the sixteenth century from Spain, was much used on the linen shirts, collars, cuffs, coifs, handkerchiefs and other articles of dress of the period. For the more elaborate articles, a gold passing thread was combined with the more usual black silk to make two-colour patterns. With the many coloured, washable and easily handled metallic threads for hand and machine now on the market, this technique is opened up with endless possibilities. It should be noted that the technique is worked on an evenweave fabric (normally linen); otherwise the pattern will be distorted.

BLOCKING
See *Stretching*.

BOKHARA COUCHING
Commonly seen on Persian embroideries worked in coarse untwisted silk. It is not normally associated with metal thread embroidery, as the laid thread is couched with itself on the return journey, so that a good deal of the couching thread is lost on the underside of the fabric. But with some of the cheaper, pliable metallic yarns, it may now be a practical stitch for filling an area. The couching stitches are placed fairly close together so that they build up to form slanting lines across the surface. The correct effect is achieved by a slightly slack laid thread with a tight couching stitch tying it down. It should not be confused with the other methods of couching. (*See Fig. 93.*) See *Couching*.

BOUCLES
See *Purl*.

BRAID
There are various important skills in sewing on a braid.

The tension should be kept so that the braid lies smoothly on the surface without any wobbles, yet is not stretched so that when the work is released from the frame the braid gathers the fabric in puckers! *Stitching* to the fabric is done by taking a stitch

91 Blackwork and metal thread embroidered coif. Early seventeenth century. (*Museum of Costume, Bath*)

92a Metal thread work on a traditional blackwork design. (*Lorna Jolley. Manchester Polytechnic, 1986*)

on alternate sides of the braid, from the fabric over the edge of the braid into the braid, following the line of the woven or plaited threads. If it is a tightly woven braid then a short straight stitch, at right angles to the edge of the braid, is used. Should the braid be too wide to take the thread across the back of the braid underneath, then one side must be sewn on first. When sewing on the second side, always start at the same end as for the first side. This keeps the pull of the braid straight. The stitches of the second side should lie alternately to those of the first side. *Russia braid (Soutache)* is best sewn on with a half-backstitch through the central indentation of the braid. (*See Fig. 94.*)

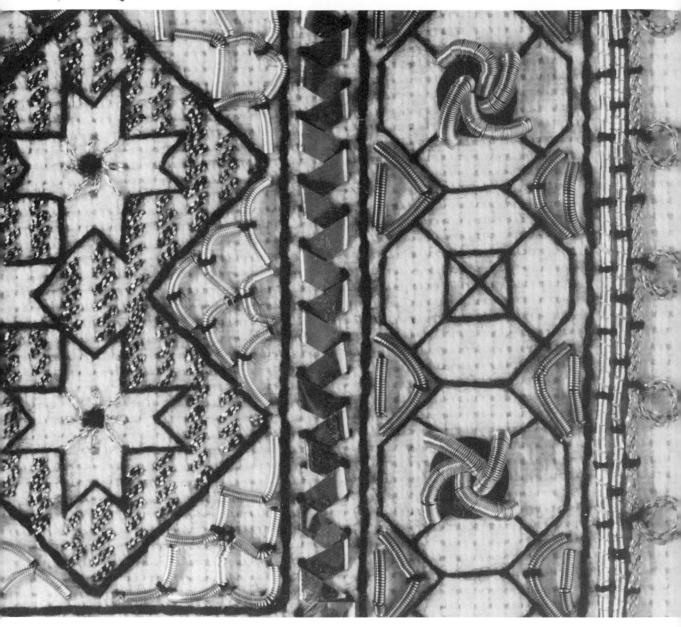

92b Detail of 92a.

93 Bokhara couching.

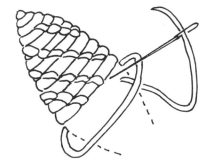

94a Russia braid sewn on with a half-backstitch. **b** Sewing on a tightly woven braid.

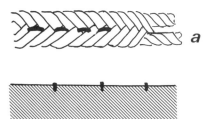

a

b

95 Hawking accoutrements. A lure, part of a set given to Sir William Pope by James VI of Scotland. Silver-gilt thread on velvet. Early seventeenth century. (*Burrell Collection, Glasgow Art Gallery & Museum*)

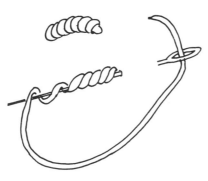

96 Bullion knots.

BRAIDING

If braid is being laid in a complicated design it is sometimes helpful to cut cardboard templates for the shapes between the braiding, so that the braid may be laid up against the card. In this way matching shapes may be easily obtained, whereas laying braids along a central tacking line can sometimes give problems.

BRICK PATTERN (Bricking)

See *Couching (Bricking pattern)*.

BROCADE EMBROIDERY

The woven pattern of the background fabric used as a design to enrich with embroidery. At the beginning of the eighteenth century, beads were used to encrust areas of the design. In the late nineteenth and early twentieth centuries, couched gold threads outlined the designs for ecclesiastical work. See *Leek Work*.

BULLION EMBROIDERY

Usually refers to the heavyweight purl embroidery used for formal insignia, badges etc. or for official uniforms and regalia.

BULLION KNOT

The thread used should have some body, so that the knot formed is full and round. The thread is brought to the surface, and the needle then placed through the fabric at the exact distance to give the desired length of knot, usually about 3 mm ($\frac{1}{8}$ in.) of the background fabric. The point of the needle re-emerges at the exact spot where the thread was brought to the surface. The thread is then wrapped round the needle seven or eight times, so that when the needle is pulled through, the length of the stitch is tightly wound with twists of thread. The twists will need to be settled into position, and the thread tightened to give a firmly twisted knot. The needle is then returned through the fabric at the original point, ready to commence the next knot. The knot can vary in length, and the minutest amount of fabric may be picked up, with the thread being covered by as many as twelve twists, depending on the thread used.

BURDEN STITCH

Traditionally, a rounded firm thread is laid in rows across the area with a space between each row. Normally, they are equally spaced. A couching stitch is taken at right angles over threads 1 and 2, the next stitch over threads 2 and 3, the next again over threads 1 and 2; and so on alternately

97 Burden stitch.

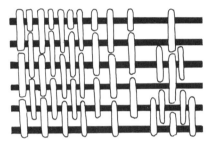

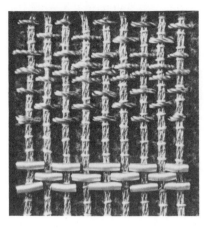

98 Burden stitch with silk and purl. (*Ann Sutton*)

99 Leopard's head, in burden stitch in different sizes of gold purl, with pearl purl drawing the lines. London hall mark used for design. (*Jean Panter*)

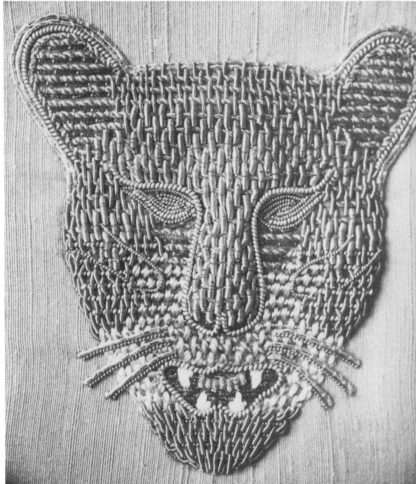

until the row is completed. This is followed in the next row by a stitch taken over threads 3 and 4, then over threads 4 and 5, and so on alternately. Equidistant spaces may be left between the couching stitches to show the underlying thread and background fabric. The couching stitch may be of silk (or any other embroidery thread), purl, very narrow ribbon, threaded-up beads, bugles or strips of leather. In the same way the underlying thread can be any heavy yarn, metal thread, cord, rouleaux, padded leather or pearl purl; but it must be pointed out that it is very much simpler if a thread that can be worked with a needle (or pearl purl which does not need to be taken through) is used, as otherwise the taking through at the beginning and end of every row is very laborious. String can be used if it is to be completely covered; in this way only the surface stitches show to give a textured area. Burden stitch may be worked with the couching stitch travelling over one or any number of laid threads instead of the two threads described here, so variations can be worked out with varied spacing to make different patterns.

BURGUNDIAN EMBROIDERY

In the fifteenth century the powerful Duchy of Burgundy covered what is now Holland and Belgium and stretched south between France and the Holy Roman Empire. The dukes were great patrons of all the arts, and one of the results was the development of the technique of *or nué* in Flanders. Like the style of painting that was fashionable there, this embroidery technique spread to Florence, where it was at its height of popularity in the sixteenth century. See *Or nué*.

BUTT

The placing of two edges together without overlapping. This can be two raw edges, or each edge can have the raw edge turned under so that the folds of the turning meet accurately together. The latter method is neater and shows less, for joining two lengths of braid or strips of leather. It is essential for wadding, pelmet Vilene and other paddings, however, that the raw edges are butted, so that extra thicknesses do not spoil the surface of the work.

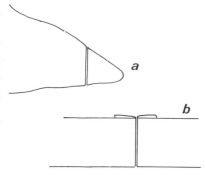

100a Butted raw edges prepared to join. **b** Butted folded edges prepared to join.

BUTTON

Decorative buttons may be worked in metal thread embroidery to enhance a fashion garment or accessory. The required shape should be worked on a frame as usual, then cut off with the necessary turnings to be made up over a mould. Care must be taken that the embroidery is in scale with the button, and that it does not become cumbersome when made up.

BYZANTINE

In AD 330 the emperor Constantine I switched the imperial capital from Rome to the little town of Byzantium, which he rebuilt and re-named Constantinople. This was the beginning of the empire and civilization known as Byzantine. Although it came to an end with the invasion of the Turks in 1453,

its influence continued throughout the east and south-east of Europe for at least another four hundred years. The great examples of Byzantine style and techniques can be seen on vestments made for liturgical use in the Greek Orthodox Church. This tradition was established during the thirteenth to fifteenth centuries in the Constantinople of the Palaeologus emperors, and was carried on into the nineteenth century wherever the Greek Orthodox rite obtained. The vestments were metal thread on a silk ground, and were nearly always decorated with figure subjects. Although the practice of embroidering Christian figures and scenes on vestments was common to both Eastern and Western churches in the Middle Ages, the tradition remained unbroken in the Orthodox church. The other branches of the Eastern church, Coptic, Syrian and Armenian (the Russian church belongs to the Greek rite), did use embroidered vestments, but apparently to a much lesser extent. There are very few pieces of existing embroidery likely to be of Byzantine origin which were made for western churches. Byzantine secular embroidery, especially on costume, was almost certainly being worked before narrative embroidery on church vestments.

Backgrounds The holy figures were always worked in gold, only the flesh and hair being in silk, normally on a dark red or dark blue silk ground both allied to imperial purple. Either colour showed off the gold figures to advantage. After the fifteenth century the colours lightened a little. The late seventeenth- and eighteenth-century figures were often worked on gold-coloured silk to give an all-gold effect. Velvet as a background was not used before the seventeenth century. Backgrounds that are now covered in silk embroidery are restorations because the original silk had rotted. The only remaining epitaphios which is entirely embroidered, with no background fabric, is the Salonic epitaphios which is a superb piece.

The laid gold was couched in silk, a

chevron pattern being the most popular; bricking, diamonds, zig-zags and other patterns were later additions. Underside couching appears to have been unknown to the Byzantine or post-Byzantine embroiderer.

Or nué was not used until very much later. Coloured couching threads can be seen after the fifteenth century for small geometric patterns, but this is not *or nué*.

The texture depended on the direction of the gold thread, or the change of the couching pattern. Different qualities of gold thread, silver, and coloured silk twisted with gold or silver threads added to the variations achieved. The laid gold was often padded with a thin layer of self-coloured cotton thread, which was completely covered.

Two kinds of metal threads were used: (*a*) a very fine wire, either pale, soft, slightly green-gold, or silver with a blueish tinge; (*b*) a very fine flat strip of metal wound round a coloured core, for which the Greek name is *chryssónima*. As in the West, it was twisted tightly so that the coloured core of the thread did not show. But it was also used deliberately less tightly wound, so that the coloured core showed through to tinge the gold. The thread was very fine, so the visible effect is a slight colouring which gives a contrast to the gold surface.

As in western Europe, it was only in the early centuries that pure gold was used. Although the thread was described as gold, it was nearly always silver-gilt.

Coloured silk was occasionally twisted with a gold or silver wire thread, which, along with a more textured appearance, gave a greater colour glow to the metal thread. The same methods were used in Romania at the end of the fifteenth century and the beginning of the sixteenth century, but with greater freedom. This colourful technique was used only in some areas, whilst others remained traditional with plain gold and silver laid work. As time went on the twisted silk and metal thread was used with less subtlety, so that by the middle of the

101 Epigonation. The Transfiguration of Christ, embroidered in gilt and silver thread on silk. Greek church, seventeenth century. (*By courtesy of the Trustees of the Victoria & Albert Museum*)

sixteenth century it had become rather coarse, and combined with the restricted colours, often only red, blue and green, was also less attractive.

By the seventeenth century *chryssónima* was out of fashion, and metal thread techniques imitated the work done by the metal workers.

The eighteenth century saw the revival of the technique, but in more natural colours used in a subtle manner. As the technique of *or nué* was never used in the East, so *chryssónima* was never found acceptable in the West.

During the fourteenth and fifteenth

102 Cover of black silk velvet, partly worked on canvas and afterwards applied. Worked in coloured silks, silver-gilt and silver thread and strips of silver. Design shows flowering plants, vine stems, animals, birds and insects. English, late sixteenth or early seventeenth century. (*By courtesy of the Trustees of the Victoria & Albert Museum*)

centuries the laid gold was turned back on itself as it reached the drawing line between filled areas, and this drawing line was depicted by a stem or split stitch in silk. Later the skill deteriorated and the gold was laid over the drawing line, which meant that there was no change of direction in the metal thread between one area and another. The drawing line was worked in silk over the metal threads. By the seventeenth century, with colour out of favour, the drawing line was marked by the actual couching stitches as the pair of gold threads were carried across the drawing line. Another method was to outline the drawing with string, so that after it was couched in gold a raised line was created to accentuate the folds of the garment etc. This, with the couching patterns, gave this plain gold style a very rich but heavy effect.

Byzantine embroiderers were certainly aware of the value of altering the angle at which they laid their gold threads, and would change the direction, if only very slightly, from area to area. But they never couched their gold to follow a curve; even the haloes were worked from side to side. It was not until the late seventeenth century that post-Byzantine embroiderers laid haloes as a circle.

During the seventeenth century

103 Purse. Tent and detached buttonhole stitch in silks and gold thread wound around a silk core. Edging of 'passement' lace, and handle of three plaited strands of gold thread. English, first quarter of the seventeenth century. (*By kind permission of the Trustees of the Rachel Kay-Shuttleworth Collection, Gawthorpe Hall*)

flat appearance which was not altered by the soft padding under the gold with laid cotton threads. Then, either from the influence of Turkish dress embroidery, or from the imported Baroque examples from the West, the work became much more raised, using felt, paper and similar wadding to pad areas under the embroidery.

During the seventeenth and eighteenth centuries, the Russians replaced the use of traditional couched applied pieces of patterns by coloured and gold brocade. With additional padding, this made the Russian embroidery of this period much stronger than the more restrained work of the style that kept closer to the original Byzantine tradition. This use of brocade was never seen in Greece or the Balkans.

gold embroidery on dress became increasingly popular in countries under Turkish rule. The threads were a fine wire thread, a new 2-ply twisted thread in gold and silver, and a 3-ply plait; the last two were both couched. They can both be seen in church embroidery of the seventeenth and eighteenth centuries. Gold bullion was introduced about the same time; the Turkish name was *TIR-TIR*, and it was used for subsidiary patterns on church work.

Up until the seventeenth century, the embroidery had a characteristic

CANVAS WORK

With the new metallized yarns, which are pliable and easy to handle, traditional canvas work stitches can be given a metallic appearance. Areas of canvas may be padded and covered in gold, silver or bronze leather, whilst purls can be sewed on to paint-sprayed canvas areas, with lurex fabrics laid under the canvas to add life to the background.

The most exciting new metal thread work on canvas is done on the sewing machine, where a well-balanced zigzag stitch can cover the canvas thread, leaving the textured fabric with its own character. Threads may be woven, applied and wrapped to add interest to the original canvas, giving a new look to the traditional mesh that has for centuries been covered with close stitchery. See *Battlement couching* and *Or nué*.

CARTOUCHE

An ornamental framework in the form of a scroll.

CATHERINE WHEELS (Spider's web)

Threads are laid to form a circle like the spokes of a wheel. These are then woven from the centre, or whipped to give a ridged appearance. These

104 Two bags. Machining on canvas with woven metallic ribbons. Cords are machine zig-zagged over string. (*Valerie Campbell-Harding*)

105 Catherine wheel. **a** A woven wheel needs an uneven number of spokes. **b** A whipped wheel can have any number of spokes, and gives a ridged appearance. **c** A whipped wheel, worked in reverse, has a smooth finish. **d** A woven wheel using threaded beads. **e** The foundation spokes of a wheel in tambour thread; the last two threads hold down a sequin.

decorative circles, which can vary in size, can certainly add interest to a design when used selectively. The choice of thread depends on the size of the wheel, but it needs to be pliable and able to pass through the fabric easily, if it is to form the basic spokes on which the filling will be worked.

CHAIN STITCH AND VARIATIONS
See *Composite stitches, Elizabethan stitches* and *Purl stitches.*

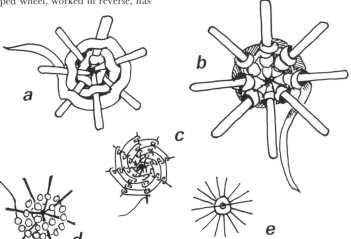

CHESSBOARD FILLING

In metal thread embroidery this refers to the laying of blocks of cut purl, as opposed to satin stitch blocks as in crewel work. See *Purl fillings*.

CHEVRON PATTERN

See *Couching (Diaper patterns)*.

CHINOISERIE

A fashion which reached Europe in the middle of the seventeenth century, for anything of the Chinese style. This did not influence the embroiderer until nearer the end of the century, when Oriental objects were imported in sufficient numbers to take their effect on design. The results did not always resemble the Chinese originals.

CHINESE KNOT (Pekin knot)

Resembles a french knot, but has only one twist to it, which is pulled tightly round the needle as it is worked. The knots are usually massed closely together to texture an area.

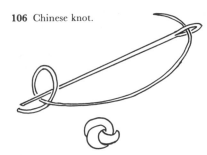

106 Chinese knot.

CHRYSSONIMA

See *Byzantine*.

CIRCLE, TO LAY

See *Couching to fill a circle*.

CLOTH OF GOLD EMBROIDERY

A Victorian technique in which gold braid was laid over a fine silk canvas (Berlin canvas), then couched down with gobelin stitch in filoselle silks.

COMPOSITE STITCHES

Composite stitches, such as raised chain band, and raised stem band can give an interesting change of texture, as a single line, a variable line, or a filled area.

The thread for the second stage or decorative part of the stitch can be any of the fine twists, passing thread, or other metallic yarns that are on the market. Waxing the traditional twists or passing threads will make them easier to handle, and less likely to fray.

Alternatively, purls can be cut to imitate the decorative parts of each stitch, giving a richly patterned result.

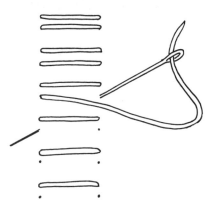

107 Composite stitches.

When purl is used the foundation bars will show, so they need to be a planned part of the design.

Bars, worked as the foundation for composite stitches that are to be worked in metal threads of any type, need to be carefully considered. (*a*) If the bars are to hold several parallel rows of stitches it must be appreciated that the metal thread literally wears out the silk, stranded cotton or fine coton perlé thread, if it is used for making the bars before the final row of the compositive stitch has been worked. It is advisable to use a well-waxed linen thread to work the bars. (*b*) The foundation should be worked in two stages, resulting in two threads for each bar, or rung of the ladder. The first thread on each rung is worked first, then, with a new thread, the second thread on each rung. In this way, if one thread breaks, the second thread is an independent stitch and prevents the foundation from collapsing. (*c*) The bars forming the rungs of the ladder need to be looser

for metal threads than they do for plain yarns, since metal threads are usually less pliable and take up more space. Small samples need to be worked, as some of the newer threads handle much more easily than the traditional ones, and so are less of a problem.

CONVENT STITCH

See *Couching (Convent stitch)*

COPTIC

Loom embroideries, usually roundels, were used to highlight parts of the tapestry-woven textiles that have been excavated from the tombs of Egyptian Christians (known as Copts) of the second to eighth centuries. The embroidery, an integral part of the woven decoration, was needleweaving. Gold threads do not appear to have been used.

CORDS

To lay or sew on twisted cords A waxed thread is used. The needle is brought up on the outside edge of the cord and a stitch is taken with the flow of the strands, between the twisted strands, into the centre of the cord. The needle is then brought up on the other edge of the cord, several twists forward of the last stitch, and the process is repeated.

108 Shows the stitches to sew down the cord. **a** The point where the first strand of a two-stranded cord is taken through to the back. **b** The second strand is taken through to the back.

To start and finish off a length of cord This is done, like the majority of metal threads, when the cord has been sewn down. The last 2 cm of cord are unravelled and taken through to the back with a sling, a stiletto having been used to part the threads of the background fabric and make a sufficiently large hole. If the cord is large, very often a neater effect can be obtained by unravelling its main strands. Assuming that there were three strands, the first is taken through to the back when it is lying under the cord, so that its disappearance does not show. A large needle may be used for this. Then, one or two twists of the cord later, the second strand is taken through, and finally the third. This method can save an ugly bulge going through the background fabric. On the wrong side, the strands of cord are unravelled and spread out. These need to be caught down on to the calico backing. It will be found that it is better to let the strands of cord run on in the direction that they were going, rather than doubling back under the sewn-on cord. Although this gives a suitable position to catch them down, it does accentuate the hole through which the cord passed to the back.

109 Cords made on the Maru Dai.

To make a twisted cord Lengths of yarn, three times the length of the required cord, are cut off and laid smoothly and evenly together. Each end is firmly bound or knotted. One end needs to be held or fixed so that it cannot unwind. On the other end, the number of strands of yarn making up the cord are evenly divided by a pencil, knitting needle or similar rod placed between them. With the yarn kept taut to the winder's left, the left hand holds the strands so that the pencil is held firmly against the secured end. The fore-finger of the right hand can then rotate the pencil at quite a speed to twist the yarn. Should a second person be set at the first end to twist the yarn as well, do make sure that both people are twisting the yarn against each other, and that one of them is not merely unwinding the twist that the other is making! When the yarn is tightly twisted and seems to be trying to double itself in places, the centre of the cords needs to be held, and keeping the cord stretched taut, the two ends brought side by side. Making sure that the cord is doubled at the centre, this twisted middle section is gradually released to allow it to twist together, working towards the two ends. When

the ends have twisted together they are firmly bound or knotted. It is a help to tie a weight on the centre to help the twisting process, but it is still better to let the cord twist in sections, allowing it to twist evenly without any little additional loops. A twisted cord can be made in any weight or size, of one type of thread or of contrasting yarns. See *TOOLS: Cord winder*.

Finger cord and plaits These also make suitable metal thread cords, but they can be rather soft and difficult to lay in firm straight lines.

Handmade cords Cords made on the Japanese Maru Dai are lovely to work with and can be produced to the individual requirements.

COUCHÉ RENTRÉ
See *Couching (Underside)*.

COUCHING (Lay-on techniques, surface couching)
The thread, threads, ribbon, strips of leather, cords, braids, narrow lengths of fabrics or yarns are laid upon the surface of the background fabric, and are attached using a second thread, by any one of a variety of methods. Couching has a number of advantages: (*a*) it gives a strong unbroken

line; (*b*) it can cover the edges of applied motifs; (*c*) by couching, threads can be laid side by side to build up a textured area and raised effects; (*d*) it is invaluable for fine fabrics where heavier threads can be couched on the surface, and not forced through the fabric so distorting the weave; (*e*) it is an excellent method for decorating pile fabrics such as velvet, where fine stitching might be lost in the pile; (*f*) it is a way of applying threads that cannot easily be taken through the fabric or that are too valuable to waste on the underside of the embroidery. Metal threads are couched by using a second, finer, working thread. The couching stitches need to lie at right angles to the metal thread, placed at a regular interval of about 4 mm ($\frac{1}{8}$ in.) apart.

The tension of the couching thread needs to be firm enough to hold the metal thread straight, and yet not so tight that it makes a 'waist' or indentation in it. To help retain tension on the metal thread, it is advisable to take a backstitch on the line which will be covered by the couched thread, every fifth or sixth stitch. Do not work with too long a couching thread: 30 cm (12 in.) is quite enough. The thread being couched needs to be held taut

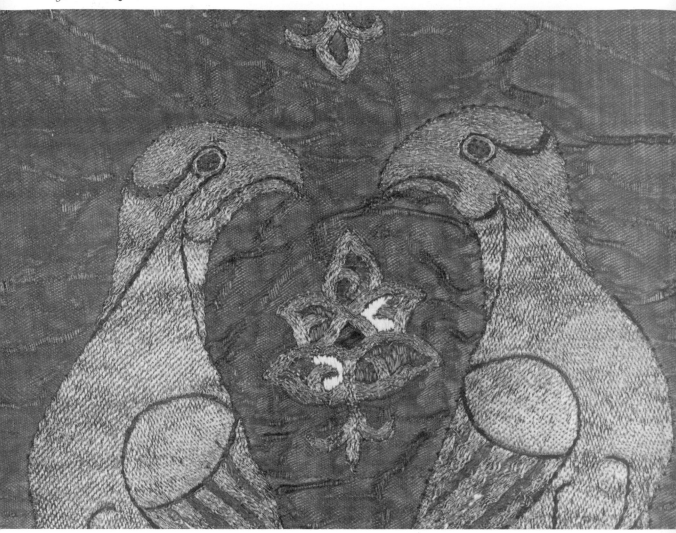

110 Fragment of robe of St Louis, from Santa Corona de Vicenza. Surface couching and split stitch. Gold and silk threads. Italian, thirteenth century. (*Burrell Collection, Glasgow Art Gallery and Museum*)

without being stretched, and turned as it is sewn to tighten its own twist. This is especially important with jap gold or jap gold substitute, as otherwise the loosened gilt paper will show the inner silk core of the thread.

The thread used for couching down the metal thread is usually stranded cotton or pure sewing silk. When one is first practising this technique it may be helpful to use a contrasting coloured thread so that it is easy to see the straightness of each stitch, and

measure an equal distance between them. With practice a rhythm is worked up and expertise improved. In certain pieces of work, where the movement of light on the gold is required to be as strong as possible, a nylon thread may be used. This thread makes an invisible couching stitch, but unfortunately is also difficult to see as one works!

Metal threads are traditionally couched in pairs, but some of the new heavier lurex threads may well be laid singly.

To begin couching Pass the selected thread over the surface of a block of beeswax. This will strengthen the thread, help to prevent it knotting, and because it is slightly sticky, will

keep it in position on the metal thread. Make a knot in the working thread, then, using a crewel needle, bring the thread up through the background to the right side, and work a couple of backstitches on the line which will be covered by the couched metal threads.

Couched metal threads may be begun in two ways. (*a*) By bending a length in half, starting with the loop and couching down the two halves as a pair of threads. The first stitch is taken from the outside of the folded thread, into the inside of the bend. Couching then proceeds over both threads with straight stitches at regular intervals. (*b*) By using the two ends from two lengths of threads. Leaving about 5 cm (2 in.) of the metal threads loose,

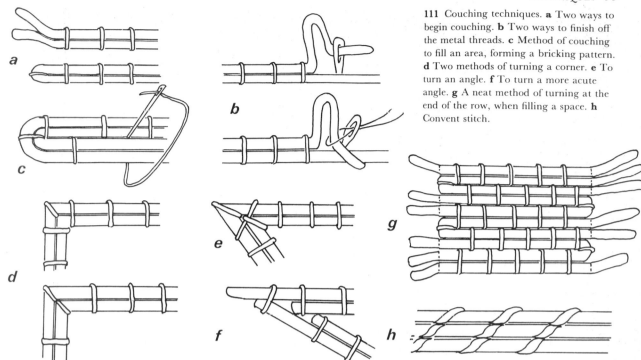

111 Couching techniques. **a** Two ways to begin couching. **b** Two ways to finish off the metal threads. **c** Method of couching to fill an area, forming a bricking pattern. **d** Two methods of turning a corner. **e** To turn an angle. **f** To turn a more acute angle. **g** A neat method of turning at the end of the row, when filling a space. **h** Convent stitch.

(this will be taken through to the back of the work later), begin to couch by taking the stitch straight up one side of the pair of threads, and straight down on the other side, keeping the stitch at right angles to the laid threads. The couching stitch needs to lie close to the metal thread on its complete journey to hold it in position.

Where threads are being couched to fill an area, the couching stitch is taken from the outside edge of the thread being couched, and down between it and the previous row. The needle should be slightly angled to pass under the thread of the previous row, so that the couching stitch pulls the thread firmly into place, with no background showing between the rows.

To finish off the metal threads First the working thread is sewn off on the wrong side, leaving about 5 cm (2 in.) of the metal threads on the right side. The two ends of the metal may now be taken through to the wrong side one at a time, leaving 4 mm ($\frac{1}{8}$ in.) from the last couching stitch, by: (a) threading it up on to a chenille needle (size 18) and taking it through the background

fabric; (b) using a sling. Thread a chenille needle with a doubled piece of heavy thread (coton perlé No. 5), then, having made a hole with a stiletto, take the needle through the hole to the wrong side, leaving a loop of thread on the right side. Place the end of the metal thread (or cord) through the loop, taking care to leave some slack on the metal thread between the last couching stitch and the loop. Then, tightening the loop from below, with a sharp jerk take it through to the back, carrying the metal thread with it. The metal threads are then unravelled, and the gilt paper of the jap gold may be cut off, leaving the silk strands of the core to be either spread out and backstitched to the backing, or stuck down.

To turn a corner (a) Take a diagonal stitch over the outside thread (a pair of tweezers, stiletto or a mellore will help manipulate the thread to a good angle), then work a second diagonal thread over the inner thread. Resume couching over both threads. (b) If the corner needs to be turned immediately after a couching stitch, or close to it, then a diagonal stitch is taken over the

outer thread only, as one is not needed on the inner thread.

To turn an angle Work a diagonal stitch over the outside thread on the angle, having manipulated a sharp turn. The second stitch is over both sides of the angled outer thread to keep a clean line. The third stitch is over the angle of the inner thread, which cannot be taken right into the corner.

To turn an acute angle The outer thread is taken round as before, but the inner thread will need to be cut, leaving 5 cm (2 in.) to be taken through to the back later, and restarted in a stepped manner below the cut end.

For an unusually acute angle Both the outer and inner laid threads will need to be cut and restarted, being taken through to the back in a stepped manner to allow for the narrow angle.

For turning at the end of a row when couching a solid shape (a) A single stitch is taken over both threads as they are turned together to return to lay the next row. (b) The outer thread is cut

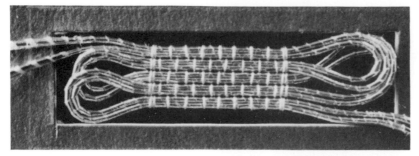

112 Couched jap gold, showing bricking pattern. (*Ann Sutton*)

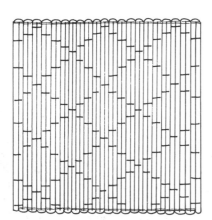

113 Couching: diaper pattern.

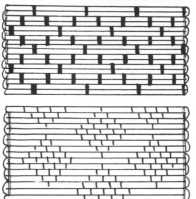

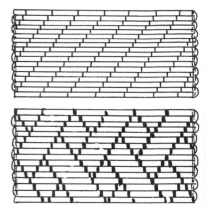

114 Couching: diaper and other patterns.

ready for taking through; the inner thread is turned, and then couched with a new outer thread on the return journey. This new thread then turns at the end of the row and is joined by a further new thread. In this way only one thread (the inner one), turns at the end of the row and each thread travels two rows, except for the very first thread. All the ends are taken

BELOW

115 Orphrey, date unknown, English, showing deterioration of design and technique. (*The Trustees, All Saints Chapel, Wardour Castle, Tisbury, Wiltshire*)

through to the back when the area has been completed. This method may use up more metal thread but it is certainly the neatest.

Bricking pattern The spacing and positioning of the stitches in relationship to each other is all-important. Bricking pattern is the basic method of couching more than one line of metal threads. Each row is couched so that the stitches lie between those above and below, lining up with the stitches in the alternate rows.

Diaper patterns Diaper patterns and other designs may be formed by the accurate positioning of couching stitches on a laid area of threads. The geometric designs, scrolling or foliated patterns should be drawn out on the background fabric. Couching stitches are then made over the metal threads as these are laid over the marked lines of the design. A small design will need only the couching stitches required by the pattern. If it is a large-scale piece the design may be couched in coloured silk or silks, and the necessary couch-

ing stitches in between can be worked in the self-colour of the metal thread so as not to stand out.

Convent stitch A couching stitch worked at an angle instead of at right angles to the laid metal thread. By positioning these couching stitches

116 Orphrey, late fifteenth or early sixteenth century, English. (*The Trustees, All Saints Chapel, Wardour Castle, Tisbury, Wiltshire*)

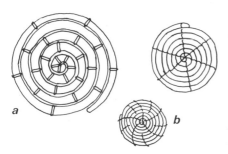

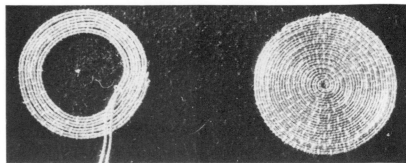

117 Couching a circle. **a** To brick a circle, the couching stitches are closer together in the centre than on the circumference. **b** Couching stitches forming different patterns.

118 Couching a circle. (*Ann Sutton*)

BELOW

119 Hanging embroidered with twisted and floss silks. Jap gold background of couched circles. Japanese, late nineteenth century. (*Embroiderers' Guild Collection*)

OPPOSITE

120 Rank badge – third rank civil (Malay, Peacock). China, late nineteenth century. Black satin embroidered with gilt and silvered alloy threads around silver cores, laid and couched with different-coloured silk threads. (*Embroiderers' Guild Collection*)

carefully, continuous diagonal lines can be built up over the area. (*See Fig. 111.*)

Bokhara couching Worked by laying a thread which is couched by itself on the return journey, so the method traditionally was not used for metal threads. See *Bokhara couching*.

Oriental couching (Oriental filling) Again worked by laying a thread which is couched by itself on the return journey, but at such an oblique angle that the couching stitch is not seen. See *Oriental couching*.

Romanian couching Of a similar working method to Bokhara couching, so traditionally was not used with metal threads. See *Romanian couching*.

Couching to fill a circle Begins on the outside edge. This ensures that the circumference is a perfect circle. If couching is started at the centre any inaccurate placing of the metal thread or threads can throw the circle so that it is distorted by the time that the outside edge is reached. If a pair of threads are being couched together, the last tight turn in the centre is made with one thread, taking the second thread through earlier. The threads on the circumference are also staggered to give a smoother finish.

Couching to fill other shapes Thought needs to go into the planning of the

121 Spray. A pear tree in silver-gilt thread and coloured silks. English, probably Elizabethan. 8 × 10 cm (3¼ × 4 in.) (*By courtesy of the Trustees of the Victoria & Albert Museum*)

couching. Consider: (*a*) the direction that the threads should lie in relation to other parts of the design; (*b*) the simplest way to fill the area without leaving awkward holes to couch at the end; (*c*) how the couching stitches should be placed to build up a pleasing pattern, and whether they should be in colour or self-colour. Very often couching round the perimeter of the shape is not the answer, though it does give the metal thread a nice change of direction. If the shape narrows at the ends, it can be better to couch backwards and forwards, laying in single lines of short lengths between the main rows to form the required shape.

It is important to plan the couching to give as continuous a line as is practicable, and so that the starting and finishing points are disguised and do not disrupt the flow of the metal.

Couching over card, string and felt These all give totally different effects. See *Padding using card, Padding using string, Padding using felt.*

Card placed under couched threads gives a clean flat area with a sharp edge. (*a*) The metal threads are couched up to the card shape, laid over the card with no stitching, then couched at the edge of the card again, continuing on to fill the area. (*b*) Guimped embroidery. The piece of card (or as it used to be, parchment or vellum) may be covered on its own with a metal thread. A fine thread gives the best results. The fine tambour threads laid in pairs are brought up to the surface at one end of the card and carried over to the other side of the shape, where they are couched down with a backstitch. The metal thread passes back over the card lying close to the first thread, whilst the

122 'Moon Landing'. Assorted couched threads. (*Flora Walton*)

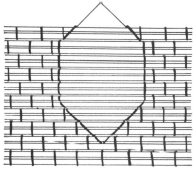

123 Chessmen. Three-dimensional bishop and knight with leather bases. Couched jap gold to follow the required shapes, with added details of pearl purl and plate. (*Mary Johnstone*)

125 Couching over card.

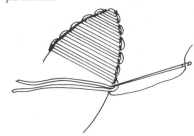

126 Guimped embroidery. Tambour thread couched over card, vellum or parchment.

124 'Girl with the Hair'. Twisted couched threads and cords of various weights and tones of gold and copper. (*Diana Dolman, London College of Fashion*)

couching thread passes across the back of the fabric, to be brought through to the right side ready to couch the metal thread, again with a backstitch. Consideration needs to be given to the best direction for the metal thread to be laid over the cardboard. The shortest distance is usually the best; petal and similar shapes work well. To lay a fine thread over card parallel to a straight edge is difficult, as the edge of the card can show through.

String gives the metal threads a strong undulating line. It can be couched over to create border patterns, drawing lines for strengthening a figure, fabric folds, architectural details and general design lines. The couching stitch needs to be up against

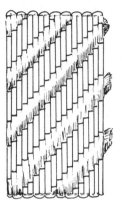
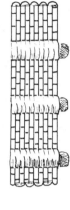

127 Couching over string.

128 Bourdon cord as padding, with laid leather and antique thread. (*Marianne Ellis*)

the string on both sides, and the metal thread needs a good even tension over the string to give a smooth rounded shape. The best known use of string for padding is for basket stitch. See *Basket stitch filling*.

Felt gives a much softer, rounder padding, and this shows in the couching results. Additional couching stitches or decorative pieces of purl or beads can be sewn on top of the shapes padded by felt, or they can be left as plain smooth padded surfaces, which give a pleasing contrast to the more textured couched area.

Open laid fillings Metal threads are usually laid to form a grid of some kind, with the background fabric showing through. Where the threads

BELOW
129 Man's cap in silver and silver-gilt thread which is coiled as it is couched on to silk satin. English, 1650–90. (*Burrell Collection, Glasgow Art Gallery and Museum*)

130 Prayer shawl (Finnish) with damascening couching. The coiling of the threads gives a filigree effect. (*Arja Salminen, London College of Fashion*)

cross, a couching stitch is made, very often in some decorative form. It could be a coloured silk thread, a cross stitch, a short length of purl or a bead. The shapes within the grid are often decorated with repeat patterns or motifs using threads, purl, spangles, beads or whatever the embroiderer can think of. See *Open laid fillings*.

Couching a coiling thread A firm pliable thread is needed, as the constant coiling could untwist a thread like a jap gold substitute. A passing is the traditional thread used. The thread is twisted into small even coils and couched into position. The result is a broader line with a more decorative finish than the regular, straight, couched single or pair of threads.

Damascening A form of open couching giving a filigree effect. The metal thread is whirled round in circular movements, covering the ground in a pleasing textural effect.

Vermicelli pattern Another form of open couching with a filigree effect. The metal thread meanders in a manner which gives an even open-textured effect over the chosen area.

131a (*above*) **& b** (*overleaf*) Stomacher. Linen embroidered with silks and silver-gilt threads that have a yellow silk core. The metal thread is couched in a circle for the flowers, with the same thread going off to provide the veins of the leaves. It looks as though these circles were started at the centre. Filigree couching background in vermicelli pattern. (*Embroiderers' Guild Collection*)

131b Detail of 131a.

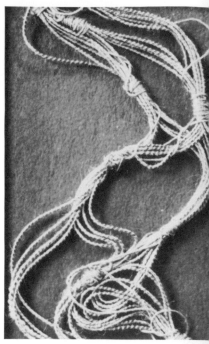

132 Bundles of threads couched with silk. (*Ann Sutton*)

Couching embellished with beads, leather, purls etc. A couched thread or cord can be tied down with a bead, piece of purl, decorative stitch, strip of leather, or ribbon in order to give it more interest, with a variable outline and changing texture. Occasionally, depending on the thread or cord being sewn down, it is necessary to couch it down before the decorative couching is added. This is to ensure that it is held firmly in position and cannot stray out of line. See *Burden stitch*.

Underside couching (point couché rentré ou retiré, pull technique) This method of couching helped to make Opus Anglicanum, 'English work', famous throughout Europe in the period 1250–1350. The metal thread needs to be pliable, as was the silver-gilt thread of that period. The silver-gilt or 'gold' background was normally laid vertically in Opus Anglicanum, in line with the warp of the material, with the silk or metal thread of the figures, animals etc. sometimes being laid horizontally to give a rich contrast. The workers seldom departed from these two direc-

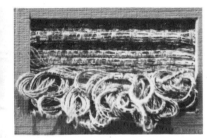

133 Jap substitute couched in layers, couched, and looped and couched, intermingled with looped threads. (*Ann Sutton*)

134 Couched leather, hand-twisted cord, ribbon, pearl purl with a perlé twisted through it and rope stitch. (*Eddie Fenwick, the Sarum Group*)

135 Couched pearl purl, alternating with strip of felt couched with purl. (*Ann Sutton*)

136 Raised chain band worked in weaving yarns over the top of couched paper beads. Beading and silk chain stitch add extra texture. (*Ann Sutton*)

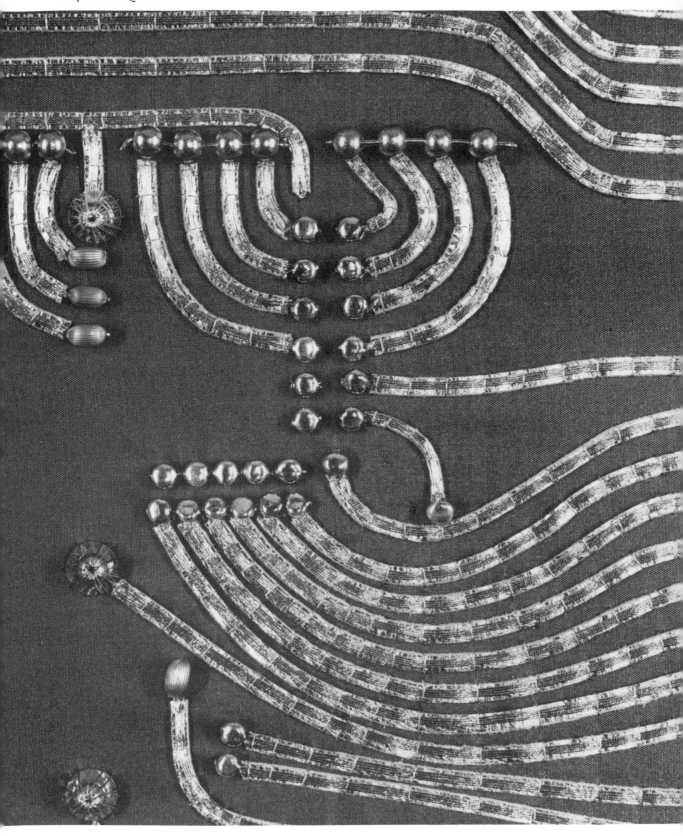

137 'Hi-Tech' (detail). The design is based on the lines and forms found in printed circuits. To accentuate the metallic lines, narrow strips of silver leather were couched down in place, then silver threads couched on top. Sequins, beads and purl were used with tiny handmade tubes of leather and silk, to indicate the details on the circuits. 30 × 40 cm (12 × 16 in.) approx. (*Hannah Frew Paterson*)

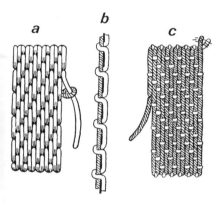

138a Underside couching, right side. **b** Shows the metal thread pulled through to the back, forming a hinge, and held in position by the shaded linen thread. **c** Underside couching, wrong side.

tions, but the changing play of light was further encouraged by the fall of the semicircular cope and the bell chasuble. The couching thread was a strong linen of about the same thickness as the metal thread. To work this method, the metal thread is laid on the background, which needs to be a strong closely woven linen, and the couching thread is brought to the surface in the usual way. The couching stitch is then taken over the gold and the needle returned through the same hole from which it emerged. Very little slack needs to be left in the metal thread, so that when the loop of linen thread is given a sharp pull, just enough of the metal thread comes through to form a minute loop which holds the couching thread firmly as it runs across the back of the work. This metal thread loop acted like a hinge on the Opus Anglicanum pieces, and the couching had a flexibility that

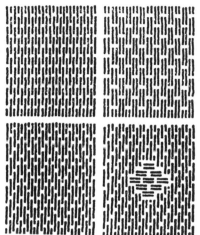

139 Background diapers worked in underside-couched gold.

140 Gold backgrounds worked in diaper patterns with underside couching.

made the copes move in a very beautiful manner, compared with the stiffness of those with normal surface couching. Underside couching also made the work much more durable, as the couching threads, being hidden from wear and tear, did not get destroyed with use. Designs worked in underside couching show up extremely well, as the surface is broken up with the shadow caused by the thread being pulled through to the back of the work. This accentuates the design formed by the couching stitches. Underside couching was used to lay both metal and silk threads.

The technique was used in Sicily, and occasionally in France and Italy, but the finest work was seen in Opus Anglicanum.

141 Cross with shadow on evenweave background. Underside couching and pulled work in Elizabethan twist. (*Jean Panter*)

142 Linen sampler with silks, silver and silver-gilt thread in tent stitch, buttonhole stitch and some raised and padded work. Formalized flowers with insects, birds and a fish. The central groups of flower heads have three-dimensional petals. Mid seventeenth century. (*Burrell Collection, Glasgow Art Gallery and Museum*)

COUNTED THREAD

With metallic threads which are both pliable and washable on the market, there is no reason why the various counted thread techniques should be excluded from use in metal thread embroidery, where they can bring a different look to the work. Such experiments can only be judged by results, and the extra glitter must not replace the skills needed to show these techniques to their best advantage. See *Blackwork, Canvas work*.

143 Detail from a Victorian panel, possibly intended for a pole screen, with pulled work techniques in metal thread. (*By kind permission of Jean Panter*)

144 Machine stitching on canvas to give pulled work effect. (*Ann Sutton*)

145 Design for pattern darning.

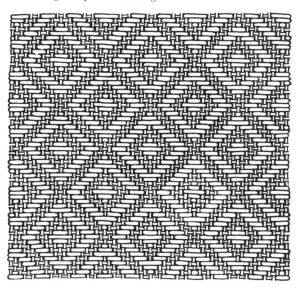

COVERING METAL RINGS
See *Leather, Wrapping*.

COVERING PIPING CORD
See *Leather*.

CRENELLATED
See *Battlemented*.

CRIMPED PLATE
See *Plate*

CROCKET
A small carved projection used to decorate the slopes of roofs or spires. It often has the appearance of a hook. Crockets may be seen on the arcading of the Butler Bowden Cope.

CROSSWAY
See *Bias cut*.

DAMASCENING
See *Couching (Damascening)*.

DARNING
Darning, like the other counted thread techniques, requires suitable passing threads, and at the end of 1980s there is a great choice of these new metallic threads. They are both stronger and more enjoyable to work with than ever before. Darning is a comparatively quick method of filling a background and can add a textural richness, without fuss, to a piece of traditional gold

146 Surface darning. The threads are taken through the fabric only at the edges of the shape, and are worked over a laid foundation.

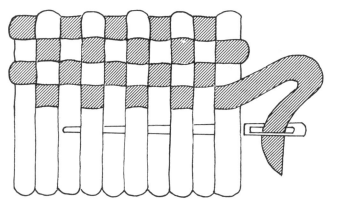

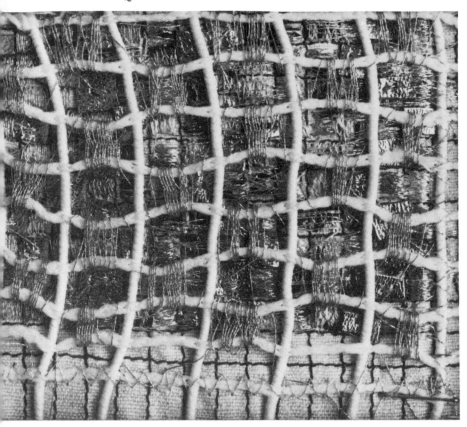

work, providing that a suitable background material is selected. A fabric where the threads can be easily counted is essential, as regular stitching is the essence of pattern darning. The various darning patterns are the same diaper patterns as used for couching laid work.

Surface darning is a further technique for adding areas of texture to metal thread embroidery.

DIAPER PATTERNS

The name given to gold couching patterns made up of small geometric shapes placed as a 'dropped pattern', to give the distinguished overall effect of diagonal lines. See *Couching (diaper patterns)*.

147 Filet darning in 'machine' thread by hand, over machine satin stitch blocks and applied leather squares. (*Valerie Campbell-Harding*)

148 Panel of Elizabethan needlework, silver and silver-gilt on linen. English *c.* 1600. (*Burrell Collection, Glasgow Art Gallery and Museum*)

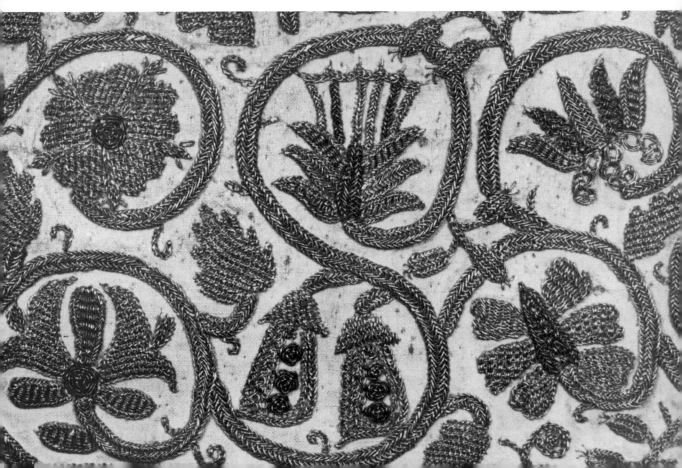

DRAWN THREAD WORK

Another technique which can be worked in the metallic threads available today. It is important to give thought to using the glitter so that it enhances the techniques.

DRESSING A FRAME
(Framing-up, Mounting a frame, Frame mounting)
See *TOOLS: Embroidery frame.*

DRIZZLING (Unravelling, parfilage)

A fashionable pastime in the eighteenth century which involved unwinding the metal from metal threads and laces in order to sell it for melting down.

ELIZABETHAN STITCHES

The embroidery was worked in silks, silver and silver-gilt threads. The imported silks were a floss silk and one that was slightly twisted. The metal threads were a fine silver and silver-gilt wire of unvarying diameter, known as sewing gold, which originated in Nuremberg. The thread was able to be made in England about 1565, when the steel draw-plate was introduced. Within twenty years wire-drawing was to become an important craft. Steel needles had replaced the old drawn wire ones, and were a great improvement. The stitches that can be seen worked in silk are chain, stem, backstitch, double running, link stitch, satin, brick stitch, herringbone, french knots, coral stitch and speckling (see *Seeding*). Some of these can be found occasionally in a metal thread. The metal thread was used in the main for buttonhole and buttonhole fillings, plaited braid stitches, raised plaited band, whipped ladder stitch, basket stitch, and interlaced knots. A couched cord can be seen for a coiling tendril pattern.

EMBOSSED VELVET WORK

The use of embossed velvet as a ready-made design, to be outlined with Jap gold thread or gold cords. The Victorians used this technique for altar frontals, amongst other things.

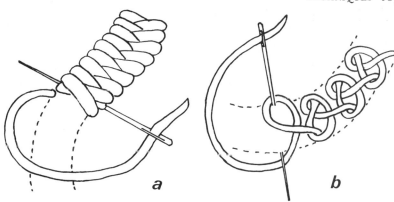

149 Elizabethan stitches. **a** Basket stitch. **b** Braid stitch.

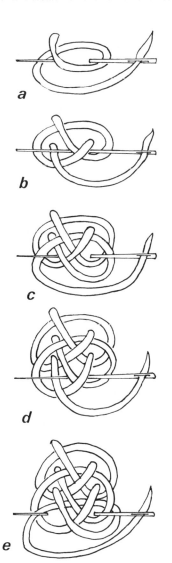

150 Plaited braid stitch. After working **e** repeat **d**; **d** and **e** are the two movements of the stitch. Use a coarse stiff thread.

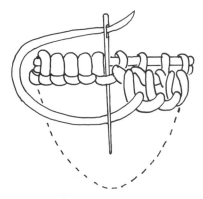

151 Detached buttonhole stitch filling. Detached buttonhole was worked as a tight, close stitch to make flower petals etc. which were almost entirely detached from the ground. It is shown here opened up to explain the working method. The foundation is two satin stitch bars.

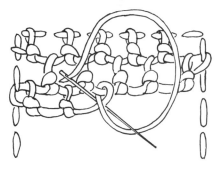

152 Knotted buttonhole filling, worked on a foundation of backstitches, round the area to be filled. For the second line, worked from right to left, the buttonhole stitches must be reversed. This is a detached filling and enters the background only at the beginning and the end.

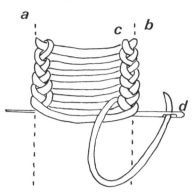

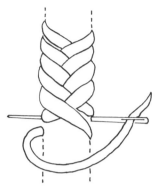

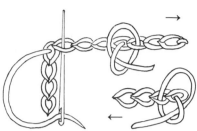

153 Ladder stitch.

154 Plait stitch, similar to basket stitch but extended rather more.

155 Trellis stitch. Using untwisted thread, outline the shape to be filled with a chain stitch to carry the stitches at the edge, as the thread never enters the background. The knots are pulled tight to give a solid filling with a slanting direction, which varies with the direction in which the stitch is worked, as the looping of the stitch must be reversed. When picking up the stitch in the row above, use the natural space between the knots. Different patterns may be built up by varying the direction that the row is worked. Spiral trellis is begun in the centre of the circle by making one chain stitch. The knots are worked round, with two knots into the loop above where it is needed to keep the circle flat.

156 Detail of a panel, possibly a cushion front, English *c.* 1610–20. Linen embroidered with silks, silver and silver-gilt threads, with silver-gilt spangles. Detached buttonhole stitch (padded in places and sometimes worked over gold threads), chain, stem, raised plaited band and whipped ladder stitches with interlaced knots. (*Embroiderers' Guild Collection*)

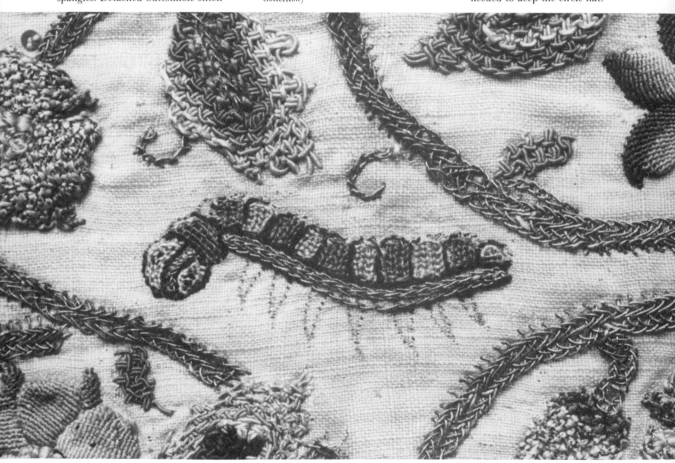

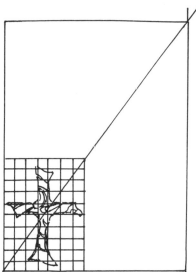

157 Bedspread, English, late eighteenth century. The sprig is worked in silk and silver-gilt threads. The stem is worked in a ladder stitch, making a double ladder instead of the more usual single one, using a passing thread. (*By courtesy of the Trustees of the Victoria & Albert Museum*)

EMBOSSING

The technique of padding with moulds, felt and hard padding. It can be seen in the raised techniques of the insignia on military dress uniform.

ENLARGING A DESIGN

(*a*) Enclose the design within a rectangle, and divide it up into squares. The more detail that is required, the smaller the squares will need to be. (*b*) Take a large piece of paper and place the design on the bottom left-hand corner. (*c*) Draw a diagonal line from the bottom left-hand corner of the design through the top right-hand corner, and on to the paper to the height required for the enlargement. (*d*) Using a set square, complete the enlarged rectangle. (*e*) Divide the new rectangle into the same number of squares as the original. (*f*) Now mark in points of the design in each square, or where the design lines cross lines of the grid. The points are then joined up, giving the enlarged design.

FAÇON D'ANGLETERRE

The term used to describe the coarser style and less detailed drawing shown in work after the Black Death of 1349.

FINISHING OFF METAL THREADS

See *Couching (to finish off)*.

FINISHING OFF BY USING A SLING

See *Couching (to finish off)*.

FLORENTINE STITCH (Bargello work, Flame stitch, Hungarian point, Fiámma)

Traditionally worked in tapestry or embroidery wools or silk threads on a suitably sized canvas so that the threads completely cover the background in upright straight stitches. The stitch is carried vertically over four strands of the canvas, with the second stitch starting two strands down from the top of the first stitch to lie alongside it. The second stitch is then laid again over four strands of canvas and back under two ready for the third stitch. This stepping pattern moves upwards in a slope for so many stitches, then downwards to make a planned pattern. Variations are made by (*a*) altering the length of stitch; (*b*) moving the stitches up and down at different intervals to alter the angle of the slope; (*c*) the use of shaded colour.

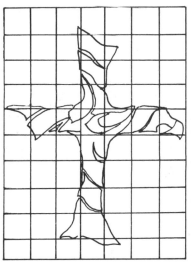

158 Enlarging a design.

159 Florentine stitch.

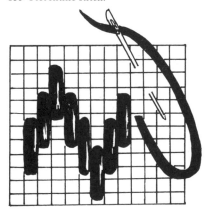

160 Detail from panel incorporating watch parts, *c.* 1970. (*Jean Panter*)

FRAMING-UP
See *TOOLS: Embroidery frame.*

FRENCH KNOTS
A useful stitch for texturing, shading and points of decoration. They need to be neat and firm. The thread is brought to the right side of the fabric and held taut with the finger and thumb of the left hand, quite close to where it came through, while the point of the needle encircles the thread twice. With the thread twisted round the needle, and still taut, the needle is taken back through the fabric close to where it emerged. The completed knot should be left lying on the surface. The number of twists used for the knot depends on the size of knot required.

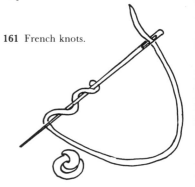

161 French knots.

This technique can be worked in a wide variation of metal threads, metallic yarns and ribbons to give interesting and rich texture. If areas of traditional gold work techniques are required, and the canvas is an unsuitable background, then these may be worked separately on calico or linen and applied as a motif on the florentine background.

When selecting metallic threads to work on the canvas, the normal canvas work rules apply: (*a*) the thread must cover the canvas; (*b*) the thread must not be so thick that it distorts the holes of the canvas; (*c*) if there are several strands in the needle, then they are all laid in the same direction when they are cut from the skein or spool; (*d*) the strands lie flat and smooth in the making of the straight stitch, which apart from looking good, helps to cover the canvas.

Florentine does not necessarily have to be worked in the traditional formal patterns; it can have a free rhythm and be used inventively. Bear in mind, however, that it is the flow of line and shaded colour that gives the method

charm, and this should be retained.

The flowing pattern could also be worked so that it faded into unworked areas of painted or sprayed canvas. These could have lurex fabrics laid behind them, to add depth and carry the metallic glint across the work.

FOLIATED PATTERN
The arrangement into formalized pattern of leafed branches and boughs. This can be seen in some Opus Anglicanum work: for example, the framework of the Steeple Ashton Cope is foliated barbed quatrefoils.

FOUND OBJECTS
In the 1960s small metallic objects were combined with metal thread techniques to create pattern and change of texture. Different-sized washers, watch and clock parts were very popular.

FOUNDATION
The threads laid across a motif or area in preparation for tying and/or couching down. This is the basic technique for many laid or open filling patterns.

FRET
Architectural term for geometrical ornament used on a flat surface, generally as a band, formed by horizontal and vertical straight lines. In embroidery, the term 'fret' refers to strapwork patterns made of braid or stitchery in the sixteenth century.

FRINGES
Handmade fringes can be made in three ways. (*a*) By *fraying* out the warp or the weft from loosely woven fabrics. (*b*) By *darning* threads back into the fabric for the depth of about 3–4 cm (1½ in.), or more if a decorative border is being worked. This method is used when the material is very fine, and frayed-out threads would not have enough weight to make a satisfactory fringe. (*c*) By *knotting* threads on to the edge of the fabric, or into a

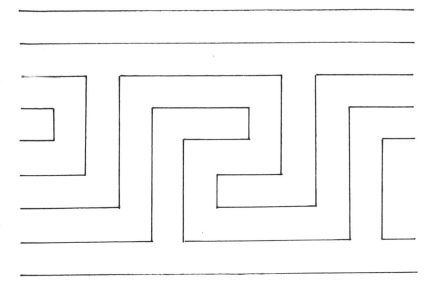

162 A running fret, seen in strapwork designs.

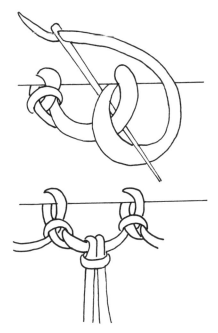

163 An edging of knot stitch to carry a fringe.

164 Fringe with sequins, purls and beads, on an eighteenth-century cope. (*The Trustees, All Saints Chapel, Wardour Castle, Tisbury, Wiltshire*)

row of knot stitch worked on the edge.

Fringes can be decorated by knotting, plaiting, wrapping, threading with beads, purl, sequins or anything that can add the richness. It is important that the threads of the fringe have enough weight to hang and move well.

FROG

The fastening made from a loop of braid or rouleau with a button or toggle.

FROGGING

The decorative loops of braid, cords or metal threads that surround frogs, and which can build up into an impressive design on the front of military uniforms; often known as Brandenburgs from the rich use on Prussian military uniforms. Frogging became a fashionable detail on women's costume in the second half of the nineteenth century, possibly as a compliment to Prince Albert, who was often seen in military uniform.

GALLOON (Golon)

The name given to trimmings on liveries and dress. It covers binding, braiding, trimmings and includes the metal threads used for the narrow lace which edges uniforms.

GEMSTONES, ATTACHING

See *Stones, sewing on*.

GIMP

Has come to mean a braid or cord with a stiffened base. This is attached in a manner suitable to its construction. See *Braids, Cord*.

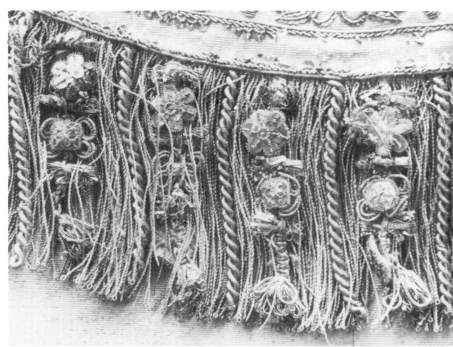

165 Stole end with garnet and a beautiful variegated fringe, 1840–50. (*All Saints' Convent, Oxford*)

GLUE (Paste, Coller)

It used to be normal practice to glue the back of embroidery, and indeed still is for badges, insignia and other formal pieces of work. On completion, white starch, gum Arabic or other strong glues were pasted over the back to give the fabric firmness, also serving to hold the metal thread or silk ends to the underside. Today, ready-prepared paperhanger's paste, bought in a bucket, is one of the glues used. Care must be taken to ensure that the glue is really dry before the work is removed from the frame, otherwise the fabric will shrink and buckle. It must be remembered that badges and insignia are worked over tailor's canvas or holland plus an additional layer of calico or linen, so that the glue does not penetrate to the right side of the fabric, where there is likely to be heavy padding as well. Earlier gold work was often worked over two layers of backing, so anyone deciding to glue the back of their work today must experiment to check that the glue is thick or dry enough not to stain the right side of their embroidery, which is often only worked on a medium-weight calico and a silk-type background.

GOLD THREAD

Gold thread is divided into those yarns that have to be laid on the surface of the background and subsequently couched (sewn) down, and those that can be used in a needle. Many which are able to be sewn with are also used as couching threads. See *Couching*.

GOTHIC

The name covering the architectural style of western Europe, which includes the periods of Early English, Decorated and Perpendicular style from approximately 1200 to 1500. The style arose from the use of the pointed arch, and its development with decoration. The reflection of this was seen in all crafts, including embroidery, where designs reflected the developments in church architecture.

GRAIN

The line of the warp, of the thread running the length of a piece of fabric. The best 'hang' of a piece of fabric is always with the grain. When the 'straight grain' is referred to, this also includes, in present-day terminology, the line of the weft (that is, the thread running the width of the fabric, or from selvedge to selvedge). Traditionally, the cutting along the weft is called cutting *across* or *against* the grain.

GRECIAN CORD

See *Cord*.

GUARDED

A fifteenth- and sixteenth-century term meaning edged with braid, embroidery or lace.

GUIMPED EMBROIDERY

The name given to the technique of couching a fine metal tambour thread over a design padded with vellum, parchment (cartisane), or felt-like fabric. See *Couching (over card)*.

HALF-BACKSTITCH

In a backstitch, the thread travels forward on the wrong side of the work and backwards to join the previous stitch on the surface of the work. In a half-backstitch the method is exactly the same, except that on the surface of the work a gap is left between the stitches, equal to the length of a stitch. The half-backstitch retains a good tension, but has the appearance of a running stitch.

HUNGARIAN POINT

See *Florentine stitch*.

ICONOGRAPHY

The representation of saints and prophets in art. In ecclesiastical embroidery, this may be seen in Opus Anglicanum. Very often the figure is identified by association with a historical symbol, such as St Paul with a sword.

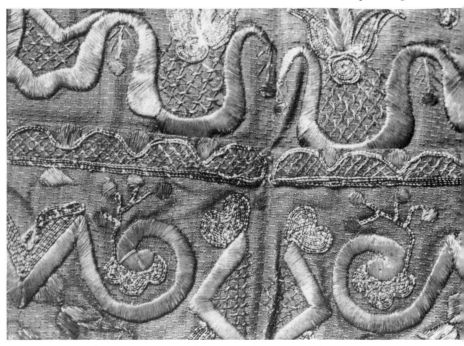

166 Man's indoor cap. Detail to show guimped embroidery, couching over (?) vellum. French, early eighteenth century. (*Embroiderers' Guild Collection*)

167 Half-backstitch.

INCRUST (Encrust)

To ornament a surface richly with another material, usually metal thread embroidery including braids, cords, jewels and lace. It implies a rich texture, often using raised work.

INTERLACED BARBED QUATREFOILS

See *Quatrefoils*.

INTERLACING

See *Strapwork*.

JANINA EMBROIDERY (Joannina embroidery)

In the late eighteenth and nineteenth centuries the Greek town of Janina was famous for its gold embroideries for costume, which were exported.

JEWELS, ATTACHING

See *Stones, sewing on*.

JEWISH EMBROIDERY

Jewish embroidery has an interesting but little known history. Jews in the Middle Eastern countries were highly skilled in embroidery, and dominated some branches such as gold work. Further west a guild of gold embroiderers at Fez was particularly skilled, as the Jews in that area had always been allowed to practise their craft. The Spanish Jews were highly skilled embroiderers, and when they were expelled the craft suffered in Spain. But as they moved on to the Mediterranean area they took their skills with them and passed them on to the local population. The embroidery worked in the Mediterranean area appears to have been produced for distinctive Jewish clothing rather than for ceremonial purposes.

Spanier arbeit The name means 'Spanish work' and refers to a technique practised by Polish Jews in the nineteenth and twentieth centuries, up until the persecution of the Jews by Hitler. On wooden frames, gold and

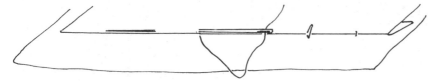

168 A fold of material being applied to a background with ladder stitch.

170 Orphrey of English embroidery, *c.* 1475. Laid floss silk secured with a silver-gilt thread trellis pattern on the upper background, and gold couched with an interwoven pattern on the lower half. The split stitch on the figure is not in the Opus Anglicanum style. (*The Trustees, All Saints Chapel, Wardour Castle, Tisbury, Wiltshire*)

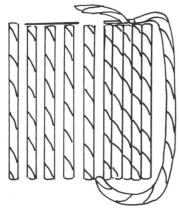

169 A laid foundation by the second method, for threads which can be used in a needle.

silver threads were wound around cotton cords. These were used for the neckbands of prayer shawls (the atarah), for kippot (yarmulkes) and for the chest bib worn by brides in Poland. There are references to Jewish guilds of embroiderers and tailors in Prague in 1741, and the Embroiderers' Guild at Prague was among the best-known Jewish guilds in the city. See also *Yemenite embroidery*.

KID
See *Leather*.

KNOTTED STITCHES
For knotted buttonhole filling stitch, see *Elizabethan stitches*. For knot stitch, see *Fringes: Bullion knot, Chinese knot, French knot*.

LADDER STITCH (Blind hemming)
In metal thread embroidery, ladder stitch is used for applying a motif when the fabric has been turned under to the wrong side, leaving a fold on the edge to be sewn down to the background. The needle comes up

171 Sampler by Miss K. Powell, showing couching and laid work. British, 1910. (*Embroiderers' Guild Collection*)

through the background and picks up the fold in the piece to be applied, at a point which is at right angles to where the needle emerged. The needle is pulled through the fold and taken at right angles again, down into the background. When the thread is pulled tight, the stitches attaching the appliqué should not show any thread on the surface of the work.

LAID THREADS
Those that are laid singly or in pairs, side by side to cover an area, on the surface of the fabric. They are then kept in position by various couching methods. See *Couching.*

LAID WORK
The laying of threads side by side to fill an area of the design. Silk or metal threads give the most exciting results because of their reflection of light, but other threads and wool can certainly be used. An embroidery frame is needed for this technique even if metal threads are not being used. These may be attached to the background by several methods.

The threads may be *couched* as they are laid. The couching stitches can form patterns of different types. See *Couching (bricking and diaper patterns).*

A foundation of laid threads may be *tied down* with couched metal, silk or other threads, with open filling stitches; or with a combination of purls, yarns, plate and anything else which makes a satisfactory pattern with a change of texture and tone. See *Open laid fillings.*

Laid foundation This may be prepared in two ways with threads which can be used in a needle. (*a*) The thread is brought to the surface at the edge of the area and laid smoothly to the other side, where a minute stitch is taken; the thread is then laid next to the first one and returned to the other side, where another minute stitch is taken. The area is filled up with the repeated long stitches. The tension needs to be relaxed, not strained, especially with silk. (*b*) The thread is brought to the surface at the edge of the area and laid

172 Sampler by Miss R. K. Evans,
showing metal thread laid work patterns,
combined with long-and-short stitch in
silk. Early twentieth century.
(*Embroiderers' Guild Collection*)

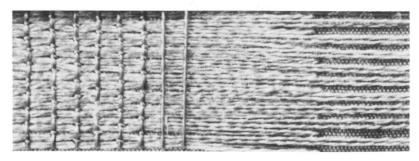

173 Silk threads laid in pairs, couched
down with imitation jap gold. (*Ann Sutton*)

174 Lurex braid laid over string and padding. (*Joyce Hill, London College of Fashion*)

smoothly across to the other side, where a stitch is taken and the thread returned to the first side, leaving a gap to be filled in, at a second stage, with another thread. In this way alternate threads are laid, and the gaps filled in with a second thread when the first stage is completed. To lay a foundation of threads which cannot be used in a needle, see *Couching (For turning at the end of a row)*.

The laid foundation may be laid vertically or horizontally, and the change of direction certainly adds interest to the whole piece. The variation in the weight of the threads which are used to tie down the laid foundation makes an enormous difference to the strength of the area created, and care must be taken to maintain the right balance throughout the piece, not detracting attention from the focal point with overweight laid areas. See *Or Nué*.

LAYING THREADS OVER FELT OR CARD SHAPES
See *Couching (Over card and felt)*.

LEATHER, SEWING DOWN
Applied leather, in the majority of cases, looks very much better with some padding, even if it is only one layer of felt; otherwise it can look very flat and thin. See *Padding (Felt)*.

To sew down leather, a fine, short needle gives the best results, as a leather needle or fatter, stronger needle makes too large a hole which shows, and can even tear away. The thread which shows the least is invisible nylon thread; otherwise a fine silk sewing thread should be used.

The leather is held in position whilst it is being sewn on either by a spot of glue or paste, which will just be enough to keep it steady on the felt padding, or by long tacking stitches over the leather shape to hold it firm. *Do not tack into the leather*, as the needle holes will show, and damage the surface of the skin.

A stitch is taken from just underneath the leather, and travels at right angles to the edge of the leather, to take a reasonably deep stitch into it. A stitch too near the edge will tear away as it is being worked, while if it is too long it will appear heavy. The stitches need to be about 4 mm ($\frac{1}{8}$ in.) apart. As the thread is tightened in the stitch, the edge of the leather will be pulled over to hide the thickness of the skin, so that only the coloured surface shows.

175a Two pieces of leather laid right side to right side, and oversewn. **b**The two pieces flattened out to show the join on the right side.

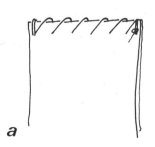

a

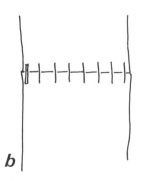

b

To join leather that is being applied Because of the shine on metallic leathers, joins do show, and it is best to try and design to the size of the skin, disguising the join with threads or natural breaks. Where the design shows a long thin strip or shape, however, there is inevitably going to be a join. Choose a spot where the shortest seam can be made, preferably not near the focal point of the design. Cut the strip of leather to be joined from the right side with a heavy craft knife, using a steel rule. Placing the edges to be joined right sides together, oversew them with a fairly deep stitch that is not too tight. Make sure that the sloping stitch is on the wrong side. When the thread is firmly finished off the two pieces of leather may be flattened out so that the leather edges butt comfortably together. This makes a good join. The two edges to be joined should never be butted and joined in position through the background, as this will always give a 'quilted', indented look, and the join will show up very badly.

Covering a metal or plastic ring with leather Cut a strip of thin leather about 2–2·5 cm ($\frac{3}{4}$–1 in.) wider than is required, to go round and cover the edge of the ring. With the fold of the leather on the inside of the ring, and the edges held evenly together, stab stitch the pieces together, making sure that the leather is stretched tight and the stitches lie as close to the outside edge of the ring as possible. When the stitching round the ring is almost complete, the leather will need to be

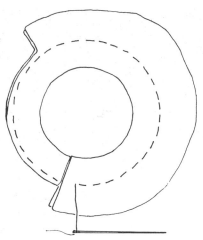

176 Covering a ring with leather.

177 Covering piping cord with leather.

178 Pleated and manipulated leather. (*Roma Mason*)

trimmed so that the edges of the join butt together on the ring. A little glue may be needed on the ring to hold the leather in place; the stitching can then be completed. The seam allowance is trimmed close to the stitches. Should the ring be required to lie flat on a background, the seam may be swivelled round to the back of the ring before the glue of the join dries in position. This leaves the front and edges of the ring neatly covered and the seam hidden.

Covering piping cord with leather A strip of leather is cut not quite wide enough to wrap round the cord. The edges of the leather are then laced together, stretching the leather tightly round the cord so that the edges nearly butt together. Do not let the leather overlap, as this causes bulk. The leather-covered cord is ready to be sewn down, using stitches that catch the underside of the covered cord to the background from alternate sides of the cord. At the ends of the cord, the leather is allowed to extend far enough to sew down into a point or round, as required, to hide the rough ends.

Manipulating leather Fine gloving kids are ideal for pleating, smocking, quilting and generally manipulation to give exciting movement, shadows and change of tone. In the majority of cases the design looks better if the pleats or folds are not carried out to all the edges of the area, but developed within the area, and can lead into a relevant technique on one or two edges where the fullness needs to be absorbed. Cut a length of leather, the

181 Pulpit fall, St James's, Dursley. Quilted leather shell couched with twist, over a couched thread cross. (*Designed by Jane Lemon, worked by Catherine Talbot, the Sarum Group*)

width being more than the height of the shape to be covered, and the length measuring twice the height. Stitch the long edge of the leather round two sides of the shape where a smooth finish is required, then start to manipulate the resulting fullness. To give clean folds and movement, the leather needs to be stretched; a pin is

stuck in to hold the tension where a change of direction is needed, and the leather pulled across to form triangular folds and variable shapes. Once the big folds are formed, they can be broken down into smaller pleats of different lengths and depths using a self-coloured thread to stab stitch in the relevant positions and hold them in place. These folds and shapes can either break down at the edges and turn into cords or threads carrying on the directional flow, be absorbed into a padded or textured area, or disappear into a point, perhaps depicting

182 Grid of woven leathers with varied threads. (*Jenny Blackburn*)

183 Fragmentary example of the work of the Leek Embroidery Society. A design of scrolling stems and formal flowers has been printed in brown, then embroidered in silks and fine wools with outlines of jap gold, on a piece of printed yellow silk shantung. English, *c.* 1880–85. (*Embroiderers' Guild Collection*)

flames. Although the metallic gloving leathers do have great stretching ability and can be manipulated in exciting ways, do ensure that the surface is not destroyed so that splits in the colour begin to show.

Quilting leather over cord or string The leather is stitched down the line where the cord is required to lie. If it is one edge of the leather, then it is stitched down in the normal manner for leather. If it is within an area of leather, then a half-backstitch is used. The cord is then pushed up tight against this line of stitching, and another row of stitching is worked to hold the leather in place over the cord. It is important that the leather is stretched really tightly round the cord to give a clear silhouette. (*See Fig. 88.*)

BELOW

185 The Master's crown of the Worshipful Company of Broderers. Late sixteenth century. (*By kind permission of the Master, Wardens and Court of Assistance of the Worshipful Company of Broderers*)

LEEK WORK

The Leek Embroidery Society (Staffordshire) was formed in 1878 as part of the Arts and Crafts Movement, and used the locally produced embroidery silks with the woven silks and brocades. Much of their work was similar to brocade embroidery. Very little metal thread was used, except as an outline to the silk floss stitchery, which formed scrolling designs of flowers and leaves in soft, rich colours from natural dyes.

LETTERING

Lettering has always been one of the embroiderer's favourite uses of metal thread work, either for ecclesiastical textiles, insignia or personal initials on domestic items or those of dress. The various techniques used have varied with the inventiveness of the embroiderer, but overall two distinct styles may be seen. In the west, the threads, cords and braids tend to have been laid to follow the outline of the letter. In Byzantine work they were couched across the width of the stroke. Modern work shows many varied treatments.

184 Orarion, the deacon's stole, with name of Petra Rares, Voivode of Moldavia, embroidered in silk, gold and silver on linen. Romanian (Byzantine), dated 1538. (*By courtesy of the Trustees of the Victoria & Albert Museum*)

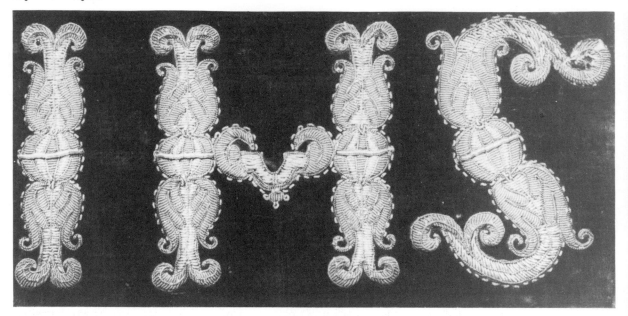

186 Fragment of velvet embroidered IMS in metal thread. English, seventeenth century. (*By courtesy of the Trustees of the Victoria & Albert Museum*)

LEFT
187 Early Victorian altar frontal. Letters in heavy jap gold thread couched over string, on a background of floss silk long-and-short stitched leaves. (*Embroiderers' Guild Collection*)

BELOW LEFT
188 Letter 'S' from an altar frontal made by Watts & Co., *c.* 1925. (*By kind permission of the Dean & Chapter of York Minster*)

BELOW
189 Cut purl over padding with pearl purl as an outline. (*Ancient Order of Foresters*)

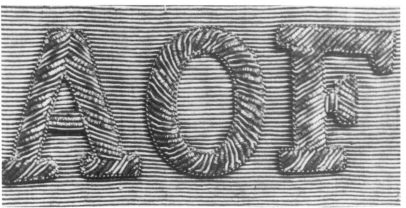

190 EIIR. Part of a cypher on back and front of uniform worn by Drum Major of the Foot Guards, state dress. (*Hobson & Sons (London) Ltd*)

191 Lettering decorates the orphreys on the set of Richardson Memorial Copes by Joan Freeman, 1985, worked by the Broderers. (*By kind permission of the Dean and Chapter of York Minster*)

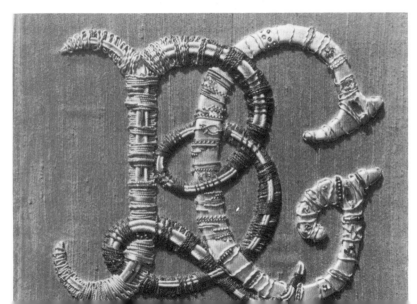

192 Lid of a box with intertwined initials. (*Mollie Collins, the Sarum Group*)

193 The design is taken from one of the thirteenth-century seals of St Bartholomew's Hospital, for an altar frontal of St Bartholomew-the-Less. The lettering is jap gold laid over padding. (*Pamela Waterworth, c. 1968*)

194 Cope. Detail from the orphreys which are decorated with two verses of the Magnificat, couched in a variety of gold lurex threads and Russia braid. (*Marion Cantrell, St Mary the Virgin Parish Church, Ninfield, East Sussex*)

MACHINE EMBROIDERY

With many metallic threads now available which are suitable for the household sewing machine, the Cornely and the Irish industrial machines, anything that may be worked in a plain thread can be given the extra richness of metallic yarn.

When using metallic threads in the machine, the tension must be loosened off, a larger needle used and a steady even pace kept throughout. Jerkiness and high speed can cause the thread to snap.

Interesting textures can be built up on the machine on most fabrics, making designs in their own right, or for enriching backgrounds to other techniques. See *Canvas work, Pulled work*.

With the use of vanishing muslin, or water-soluble fabric (now available for both hot and cold water), both formal patterned and freely stitched lace can be made on the machine. Care must be taken that enough stitching is done to link and hold the various areas together. See *Water-soluble fabrics*.

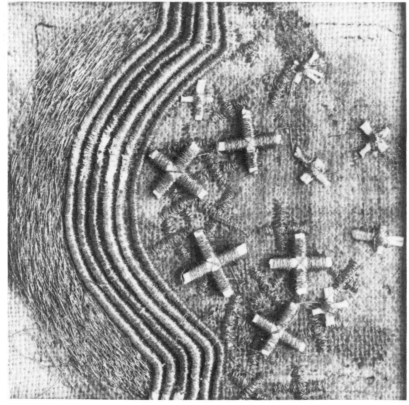

195 Cushion. Detail of painted muslin background with machine zig-zagged pulled work. (*Marian Murphy, Urchfont Manor City and Guilds Course*)

196 Machine embroidery with metal thread over string, sections of rug canvas and plastic crosses. Zig-zagged with a sideways movement to build up solid areas. (*Valerie Campbell-Harding*)

MICA
See *Shisha glass*.

MOTIF
A unit in a design. It may well be more convenient to work it separately on a small frame, and then apply it to the main work, either flat or over additional padding. There are two methods of applying a motif. (*a*) The calico or linen backing and the background fabric are trimmed away, right up to the stitching worked on the motif's outer edge. The motif is then attached to the main piece of work by a stitch taken over the raw edge at regular

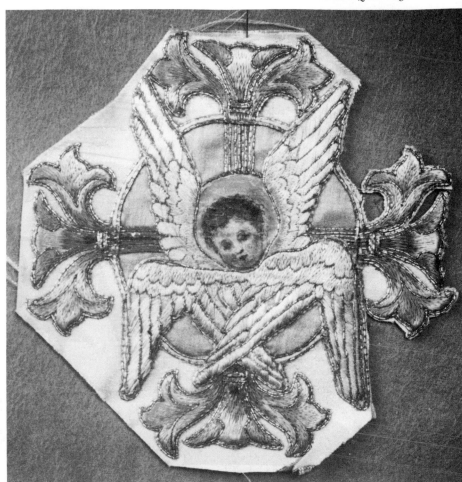

197 Sequin waste with machine zig-zag. (*Valerie Campbell-Harding*)

198 Angel motif with painted face, half cut away ready for mounting. (*All Saints' Convent, Oxford*)

intervals. A thread, threads or cord are then couched to cover the raw edge of the motif and the join. (*b*) The calico or linen backing is trimmed away to the stitching worked on the motif's outer edge. The background fabric is trimmed to leave a 2 cm (¾ in.) turning beyond the motif's outer edge. The turning is snipped so that it will turn back neatly all the way round, right back to the edge of the embroidery. The turning is over-sewn into position on the back of the motif, which is then ladder-stitched into position on the main frame. This method should not require a couched line to conceal the join. (*See Fig. 199.*)

MOUNTING A FRAME
See *TOOLS: Embroidery frame.*

NEEDLEWEAVING
Traditionally worked on linen, need-leweaving has no connection with metal thread embroidery, but with the modern metallized threads available there is no reason why they should not be used for needleweaving. It is neces-sary to do sample pieces to check (*a*) the weight of the metal threads on the woven threads over which they will be worked; (*b*) the number of strands of metallic yarn required to give a good woven result; and (*c*) that the metallic yarn does not cut or wear

the strands that it is weaving. Areas of needleweaving may be incorporated with traditional gold work by laying blocks of satin stitch bars, which are then worked as a surface stitch to show the background through, or as a base for weaving in ribbons, leather or cords. See *Composite stitches (Bars).* (*See Fig. 200.*)

NET EMBROIDERY
Darning techniques with metal threads can be used on all sizes of net or netting, either as a transparent fab-ric or to remount on to background fabrics. The main problem with this type of work is the finishing off, so that thickened areas of thread or loose ends

199 Cope. Angel and eagle motifs, with *fleur de lys* embroidered on linen in long-and-short stitch, laid and couched metal threads and stem and chain stitch lines. The motifs are mounted on red velvet with a couched gold thread to cover the edges. The scrolling line is gold thread. Cope from Great Bircham, later made into an altar cloth. 1480. (*Norfolk Museum Services: Strangers' Hall Museum, Norwich*)

200 Poppy heads. Needleweaving in
metallic thread on pleated and pieced
background textured with beads. (*Ethel
Holloway, London School of Fashion*)

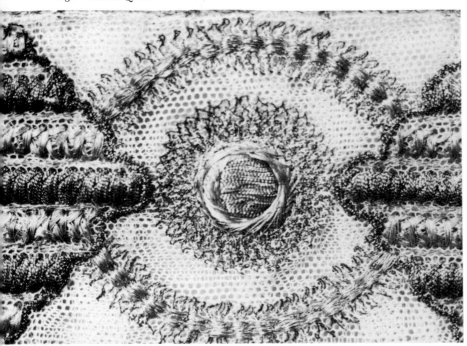

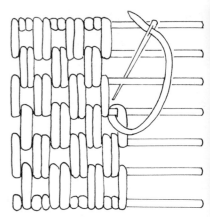

203 A surface filling over a foundation of bars, worked by alternating a stem stitch with an outline stitch (the thread taken the other side of the needle).

201 Dress trimming net stitched with metal threads, *c.* 1900–1915. (*Embroiderers' Guild Collection*)

LEFT
202 Detail from teazle panel. Free stitchery and beading on net. (*Flora Walton*)

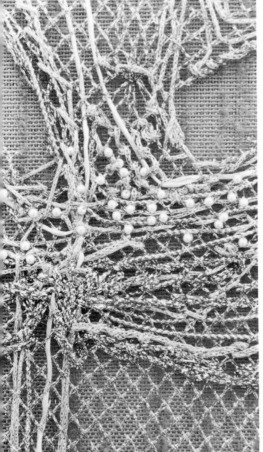

204 Ceylon stitch is started over a long line of thread, but it could work just as well over a row of small backstitches. It is taken through the fabric at the edges. It can be closely worked or spaced.

of yarns do not spoil the finished effect. Where possible, threads must be taken through to the edge of the work; if there is a dense, solid area of the design, then threads may be started or finished on the back of that part. Fine threads may be run into the backs of heavier yarns. If all else fails, a thread may be doubled back on itself and whipped with an invisible thread so that the double thread is no thicker than the single thread.

Gold nets may be incorporated into open laid fillings; they can also be used for applying over a laid silk area, or for adding texture to the background.

NUIHAKU
Japanese technique which combines applied gold leaf with embroidery.

OPEN FILLING STITCHES
Open filling stitches can give areas of

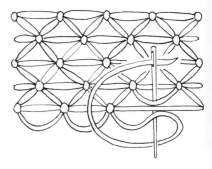

205 Diamond filling stitch is worked over a foundation of laid bars, using a coral knot to tie the travelling thread into diamonds.

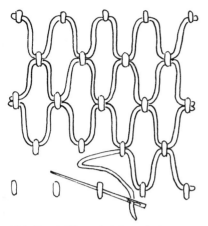

206 Cloud filling stitch is worked on a foundation of small stitches which are worked in rows, lying alternately to form a diaper pattern.

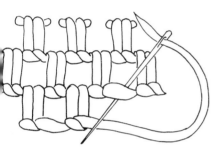

207 Open buttonhole filling, spaced, is worked on a foundation of small backstitches, and taken through the fabric at the edges. The buttonhole stitches can be worked with three or four stitches to a block, as required.

208 Laid ribbon, with gold passing thread caught with a lazy daisy on the diagonal. (*Ann Sutton*)

texture to gold work, and as the majority of the stitching is surface work over foundation threads or stitches, it is eminently suitable to the technique.

OPEN LAID FILLINGS

The decorative laying of threads in a repetitive pattern, often a grid, to allow the background to show through. The couching 'stitch' usually adds to the decoration and may be a contrasting silk, short length of purl, bead etc. The design can be built up with additional threads or small motifs within the grid.

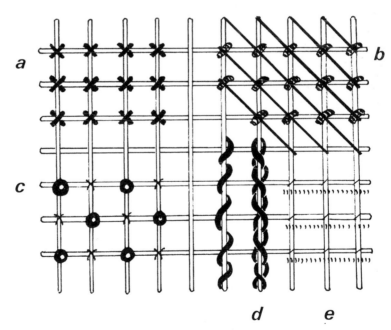

209 Open laid fillings with threads laid vertically and horizontally. **a** Tied with a contrasting thread in cross stitch. **b** An additional contrasting thread laid on the diagonal, and all three threads tied at their intersection with a piece of cut purl. **c** A sequin, fastened on with a small bead, ties down alternate intersections. **d** Raised honeycomb filling. **e** Laid threads tied at intersections and pearl purl laid in one direction only.

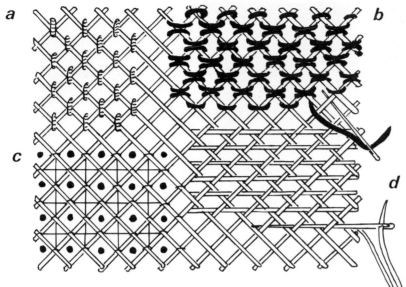

210 Open laid fillings with threads laid diagonally. **a** Tied with cut purl.
b Twisted lattice. The foundation threads should be darned over and under each other to interlace. The second or contrasting thread then weaves in and out as shown. **c** A finer vertical and horizontal line is added to build up the pattern, with a bead sewn into the empty spaces between the original foundation threads. **d** Honeycomb fillings. The diagonal threads are laid first in one direction, then in the other, without interlacing. The horizontal thread is woven in and out through the threads.

OPUS ANGLICANUM

The great period of English embroidery, which was well established by the middle of the thirteenth century and lasted until the middle of the fourteenth century, when many skilled embroiderers and designers in the professional workrooms died as a result of the Black Death. The period of Opus Anglicanum is usually dated as 1250–1350, when the standard of workmanship was exceptionally high.

The embroideries were ecclesiastical, with copes being the most important pieces. Much of the work was destroyed during the Reformation, but luckily it was held in such high esteem all over Europe that it can be traced in the early inventories as 'English work', which always referred to embroidery, rather than any other craft. It was often given as gifts and was highly prized.

Materials A background of fine linen, mounted over a backing of coarser linen, was in general completely covered with laid gold and silk stitching. Velvet was used as a background in some cases. This was mounted over a backing of linen, and fine linen was laid completely over the velvet. The design was marked out on this, and all the work took place through the three layers. This prevented the fine gold or silk threads becoming lost in the velvet pile. When the embroidery was complete, the surplus linen was cut away to expose the velvet background. These interlays were so well handled that it is difficult to see signs of them except in the worn areas of the motif. In one case (an orphrey of *c*. 1350 in the Victoria & Albert Museum) bright rose-pink silk was used for the interlay. Silk, which was also backed with linen, enabled the gold to be worked more freely within the design, since the silk could be left as a background.

Threads The gold metal thread was silver-gilt. It was made by covering a fine strip of silver with gold, and then winding it round a silk core. Silver thread was also used; this too was a fine strip wound round a silk core. Metal threads varied in thickness. Silk was almost all floss, which was divided into strands of varying thickness as required for different areas of the design. Comparatively thick silk was used for the drapery, but for the faces and hands the silk was divided down to very few strands. For this reason, they are nearly always more threadbare than the draperies. The dyes were varied natural dyes with tones of indigo, greenish-yellow, and reddish-fawn the most popular. The black dye has caused the silk to rot, just as much of the outlining black silk stitching has perished. Linen threads were used for underside couching of the metal threads, and for padding lines of raised gold.

Ornamental materials Often used for further enrichment. Pearls, both large and the smaller seed pearls, were used in abundance. Orphreys, borders, and hoods of vestments were lavishly decorated with seed pearls. In addition, coloured beads, enamel, plates of gold, stones and gems were used. Few of any of these remain on existing

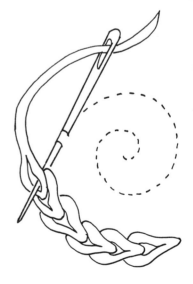

211 Split stitch. The needle pierces the working thread at a point near to where it emerges from the background.

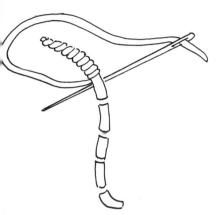

212 Overcast stitch. A thread is run along the line to act as a padding. The stitch that covers it picks up as little of the background as possible so that it is well rounded.

213a Basis composed of scrolling stems.
b Basis composed of geometrical panels.
c Basis composed of architectural framework.

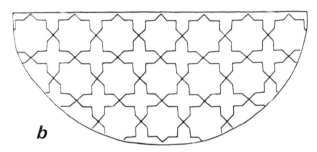

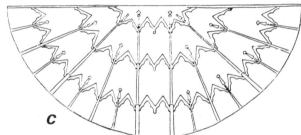

work, but evidence may be seen of their presence, and the inventories make repeated reference to them.

Stitches Underside couching was used for couching metal threads, and in some cases silk threads. See *Couching (Underside)*. Silk threads were worked in split stitch. Stem, overcast, plaited stitch, cross and tent stitch are occasionally used. Satin stitch and french knots are very rare. Surface couching and laid work, tied down with a trellis pattern, are found on the throne in the 'Adoration of the Magi', on the back of a velvet chasuble which can be seen in the Metropolitan Museum, New York.

Articles Articles decorated with embroidery were copes, chasubles, dalmatics, amices, stoles, maniples, mitres, buskins, sandals, altar frontals, dossals and fair linen cloths.

Designs The copes had the largest field for design, and the development

of the framework needed to link the different motifs can be seen in the diagrams. The Jesse Cope, based on the tree of life, has a scrolling design springing from the recumbent figure

214 Shows the change of direction in the laid threads, vertical for the background and horizontal for the motifs.

215 Butler Bowden Cope, in red velvet, showing the figure arcaded, with three crockets on top of the arch, and four twists in the foliated arcading. The small white silk areas are the underlay for the pearls that have been lost or removed. These were on the crown, the lion's masks, and the acorns. English, early fourteenth century. (*By courtesy of the Trustees of the Victoria & Albert Museum*)

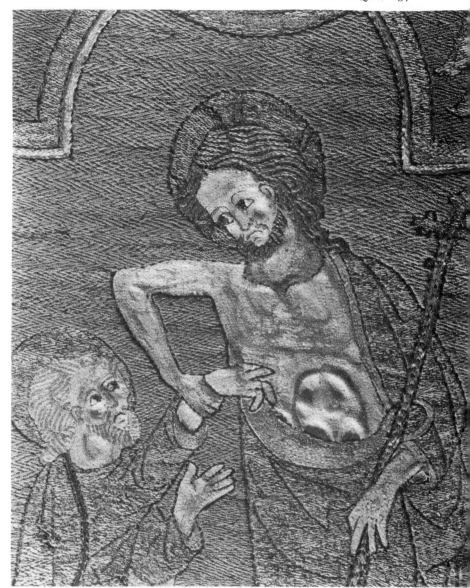

of Jesse. The curving, interlacing branches bearing undeveloped leaves and flower buds form a setting for figures or animals set within the branches (late thirteenth to early fourteenth century). This developed into repeating geometric shapes of circles, barbed quatrefoils or eight-pointed stars, which were filled with figures of saints or scenes from the New Testament (middle to late thirteenth century). The architectural framework for the designs can be seen in some work at the end of the thirteenth century, and was in common use at the beginning of the fourteenth. It continued in use until Opus Anglicanum died out. The architectural arcading fitted well into the shape of the semicircular copes, with the constantly recurring columns for the most part radiating from a central point at the neck edge, reminiscent of a cathedral rose window and reflecting the Perpendicular architecture of the day. Each figure or scene was set within an arched niche in a well planned shape. The arcaded framework developed to suit the embroiderers' skills. At first it was realistic, showing simple stone columns, carved capitals and arches. But these were replaced by columns of twisted branches bearing oak leaves and acorns, or intertwined serpents whose heads spread to form the base of the columns. Lion masks or foliated human masks (the Green Man) were used to form the capitals or junctions in the tracery.

The similarity between embroidery designs and the illuminated manuscripts and books cannot be missed.

Characteristics of Opus Anglicanum
(*a*) The strength of the drawing of the figures, which had much more movement in them than their European counterparts. The rather large heads, hands and feet added to the importance of each figure. The heads are worked in split stitch which follows the contours of the features, across the forehead, down the nose and back to follow the line of the brow. The cheeks were worked in a spiral which added to the form. (*b*) The large protruding eyes, which had black pupils stitched spirally with black split stitch. (*c*) The unrealistic colour of the hair, either brown and yellow, green and yellow,

216 Syon Cope, figure of St Thomas. Coloured silks, silver, and silver-gilt thread on linen. The cope is unusual at this period as the linen ground is completely covered in underside-couched red and green silk. It was more usual for the background to be underside couching in silver-gilt thread. (*By courtesy of the Trustees of the Victoria & Albert Museum*)

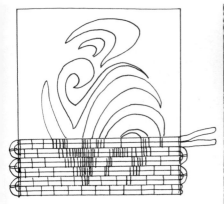

217 *Or nué.*

blue and white or black and white. Hair and beards were worked in alternate lines of light and dark colours. (*d*) The split stitch on the draperies, following the direction with contrasting tones to throw up the form of the fabric and figure. (*e*) The use of underside couching, which gave the work the movement and richness for which it became famous. (*f*) The use of black silk outlines.

The basic designs were an important feature of the work but were only a framework for the main subjects, which also helped to identify the work as English. Internationally revered saints were joined by English saints like St Edmund of Bury, Edward the Confessor, and St Dunstan. Favourite subjects, as in Europe, were figures of Christ, the Virgin and Child, and the Apostles. These filled the circles, quatrefoils and the arched niches. But for the spaces in between a wide selection of subjects was drawn: angels playing musical instruments, seraphim on wheels, birds and beasts including heraldic lions. (Animals, birds and plants, many recognizable from the bestiaries of the period, were favourite sources for embroidery design.) Identification was also helped by the inclusion of heraldic devices or coats-of-arms on some pieces. Lettering appears in some cases where the subject cannot be recognized by an appropriate symbol, and is in the Lombardic style. This is used in a similar way to the manuscripts of the period, with

abbreviations for certain words which regularly reappeared.

OPUS COLONIENSE

Work made in Cologne. With England, the Rhineland formed the other centre where fine embroidery was

218 The betrayal in the garden. The Westminster Chasuble, so called because the embroidery is derived from two vestments formerly used in Westminster Abbey. Fifteenth century, Flemish. (*The Trustees, All Saints' Chapel, Wardour Castle, Tisbury, Wiltshire*)

219a & b St John and St Anne the Evangelist: to be mounted on the orphreys of a cope to mark the nine-hundredth anniversary of the church of St Mary, Harrow-on-the-Hill. The actual figures of the saints are worked in *or nué*, over the finest size of imitation jap gold thread on linen backing. The stitching is carried out in a single thread of stranded silk. The 'castles' were worked in a single strand of crewel wool, with a little knitting yarn 'pulled out'! The canvas work was then stretched, turned in and mounted on the linen backing of the saints' figures. (*Rosemary Priestman*)

being worked in the fourteenth century. The two names became synonymous with sought-after embroidery. The great differences in the work were that: (*a*) underside couching was not used; this made the vestments much stiffer and less effective in reflecting light; (*b*) the drawing and posing of the figures was not so strong, nor so dramatic; (*c*) although split stitch was used for the silk, it was not worked in such an inventive way. The Cluny Museum in Paris has an altar hanging and some orphreys in Opus Coloniense.

OPUS PHRYGIUM

See *Auriphrygium*.

OR NUÉ (Burgundian embroidery, Italian shading)

A method of laying a gold thread, or pair of gold threads, to completely cover an area. The coloured design is painted on to the fine linen backing; the gold threads, using the best quality available, are laid in pairs, from side to side, beginning at the bottom. Each area of colour has its own length of waxed silk threaded into a needle, so that the couching is completed on

220 Stole end. Raised work on velvet, leather and *or nué* with french knot seeding, to match the Dean's cope. One of set of five. (*Designed by Jane Lemon, worked by Mollie Collins, the Sarum Group. By kind permission of the Dean & Chapter of Salisbury Cathedral*)

221 *Or nué* using fine ribbon as a couching thread. (*Sheila Miller*)

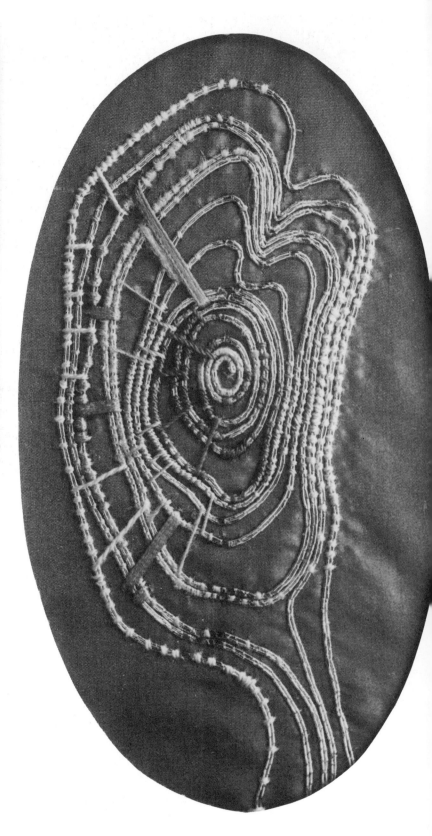

each row as it is laid. The coloured silk is taken over the gold thread as often, and as closely, as is required by the coloured design drawn on to the linen background. Areas of gold that do not require any colouring are couched either in self-coloured silk or transparent thread. The skill is to lay the metal threads absolutely straight, and close to each other, so that no glimpse of the linen background can be seen. To achieve this, a single strand of silk is used. This may be very slow, but the

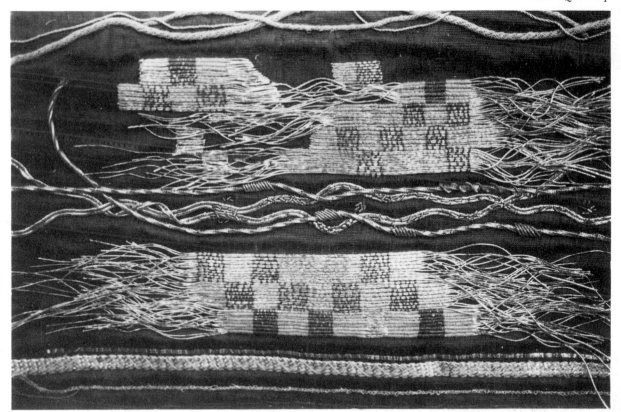

222 Panel. *Or nué* blocks leaving jap gold to fringe. Couched lurex cord and braid with purl. (*Ethel Holloway, London College of Fashion*)

223 Sampler. *Or nué* technique laying lurex cord. (*Joyce Hill, London College of Fashion*)

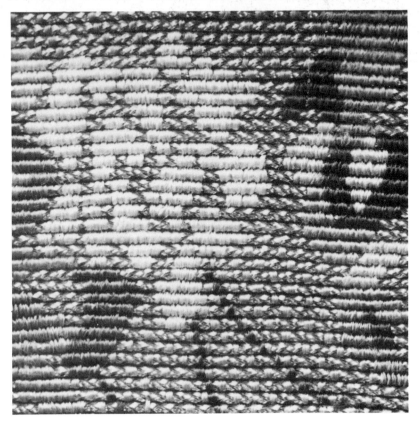

fine thread allows the next gold thread to be laid closely to the first. If several strands of a thicker thread are used to couch, they may cover the gold more quickly, but they force the next gold thread to be laid away from the first. Problems are found when subsequent areas of self-coloured background in the same row are being couched and the gold threads will not lie snugly together unless they are taken off the straight.

The style of *Or nué* arose from the painting and enamelling that was fashionable in fourteenth-century Burgundy.

False or nué With the speed of life at the end of the twentieth century, experiments have been made both to speed up the technique and to give it a new look. For example, jap gold substitute is being laid on canvas, which not only brings up the scale of the threads to a much coarser approach, but also helps the worker to keep the laid thread straight. Lurex cords are also being used, again on canvas, which gives an added texture to the work.

These new approaches cannot be compared to the real *or nué*, but they certainly have their uses on some articles and serve the purpose of keeping the technique alive.

ORIENTAL COUCHING (**Oriental filling**)

A laid thread is couched by itself on the return journey, but with such a long oblique stitch that it is hardly discernible in a solid area of laid silk threads.

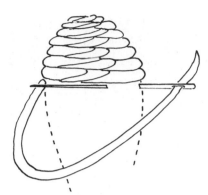

224 Oriental couching.

225 Tacking over card padding.

PADDING

The placing of an underlay before couching, stitching, or applying leather or other materials. There are several methods of preparation to give different appearances to the raised work. Try to use the same colour padding as the thread that will be covering it.

226 Pair of woman's slippers, Turkey or North Africa. Worked for the European market, mid nineteenth century. Red velvet embroidered with silver-gilt thread and check purl laid and couched over cut card and cotton threads. (*Embroiderers' Guild Collection*)

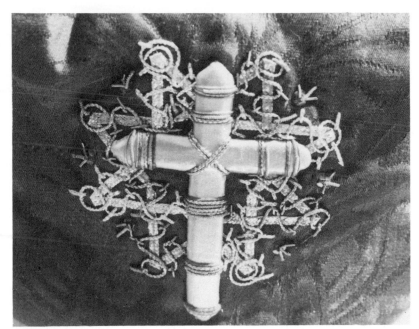

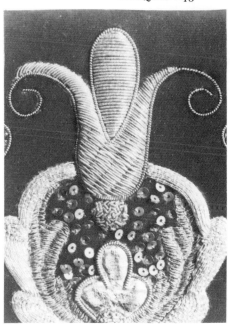

227 Detail of alms bag showing cross padded with layers of card couched with assorted metal threads. (*Audrey Chorley. St John The Baptist Church, Tisbury, Wiltshire*)

229 Purl couched over felt to give raised area on velvet. (*Mollie Collins, the Sarum Group*)

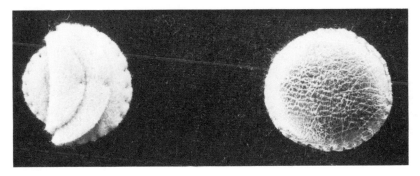

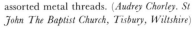

228 Three layers of felt padding covered with leather. (*Ann Sutton*)

Card, parchment or vellum When this is to be covered by tambour thread couched over the card only, to form an isolated shape, the card needs to be cut very slightly smaller than the design. This allows the gold thread to lie over the card without enlarging the design. The card shapes are cut with smooth edges. They can have a layer of felt stuck over them, if required. This takes the hardness off the surface, but still gives a reasonably crisp edge, as long as the felt is trimmed back to the edge of the card. The card may be either glued with a dry paste into position on the background, or held in

position with one or two long tacks over the shape. Do not tack through it, as the needle holes destroy the surface and may show. As the threads are couched over the cardboard shapes, cut and remove the tacking stitches so that they do not spoil the surface of the metal thread. The card may be glued together to make different heights of padded areas.

Felt May be used as a single layer or built up as a rounded shape. This is the normal method for padding leather, or raised couched areas. For an area of applied leather, the top piece of felt (that nearest the underside of the leather) is cut a fraction smaller than the leather, so that it will not show at the edges. It will in fact

stretch a little as it is being stitched on over the rest of the padding, so will end up the same size as the leather shape, which will have enough stretch in it to pull over the felt comfortably, sitting so that the padding comes up to the edge of the leather, but does not show. Below that is a slightly smaller piece, and if required a third and fourth shape may be cut, each of the same shape, but slightly smaller than the one above it. Three layers of felt are usually sufficient, but it depends on the design and the thickness of the felt. By having the smallest layer at the bottom and placing a slightly larger one over it, a smoother surface is prepared for the leather or couched thread than if the order were reversed. The layers need to be sewn into position before being covered.

For highly raised blocks of metal thread work, the gold work is prepared over one layer of felt on a small frame, then applied to the raised area that has been sewn into position on the main frame. Nine layers of thick felt, all cut exactly same size, were cut to pad each section of the fragmented cross on the festal frontal in Salisbury Cathedral (1984). Because steep straight sides were required for each section they had to be faced with strips of leather or braid to cover the felt, after the application of the embroidery on the top. Some ends of threads or cords were left to carry on over the leather sides and down on to the background.

In the past leather has been used for padding, and this is handled in a similar way to felt or card.

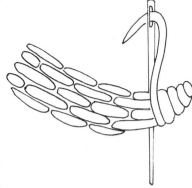

230 Padding with stitches.

231 Sewing on string padding.

Stitching Stitching with a thick cotton or wool thread, yellow for gold threads, grey-white for silver, may be used for padding. A running stitch which picks up only a minute bit of the background may be used. Each row should be bricked with the preceding row. This padded area can have a row of satin stitches placed over it, or satin stitch may be used on its own. If satin stitch is being worked it is much easier to begin the shape at the smallest point, and increase the length of the stitch as required, rather than the other way round. Stitching is rarely used for padding under metal threads now, as there is a wide selection of felts and strings that can fulfil most purposes.

Wadding or wool Occasionally used for a motif that has been worked separately. Having been completed, the motif is trimmed to its outline and applied to the main background, leaving a small gap through which the wool or wadding can be pushed with tweezers or a stiletto. This was a traditional method used in stumpwork. It gives a much more moulded finish, if carefully handled, then layers of felt.

232 Leather, plate and ribbons couched over string. (*Roma Mason*)

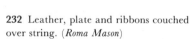

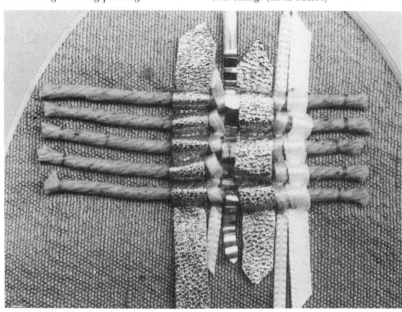

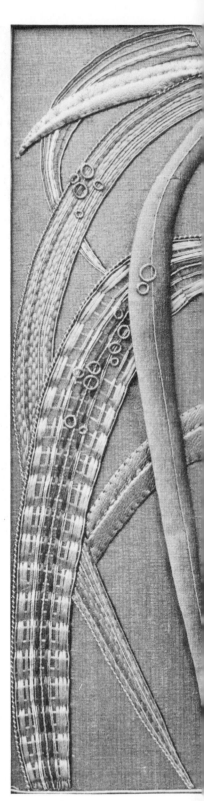

233 Leaves; three-dimensional, padded with pelmet vilene. (*Marianne Ellis*)

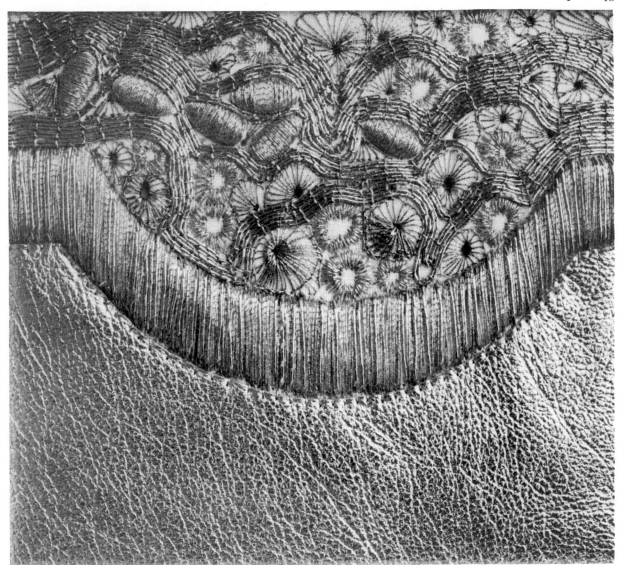

234 Detail of bag. Satin-stitched melon seeds with couched jap substitute. Border of satin-stitched pelmet vilene, with gold leather. (*Valerie Campbell-Harding*)

String String of various sizes is used for basket stitch filling, for padding patterns under laid work, for quilting leathers, covering with purls and for wrapping. The string needs to be closely twisted with a smooth hard surface. A knotted thread is taken through the string about 1·5 cm (½ in.) from the end, and wound round two or three times. The needle is then taken through the string to hold the

whip stitches firm. The rough end of string is trimmed off, ready to be sewn in position, and the end is sewn firmly down with a couple of stitches. Couching stitches are then taken into the string on alternate sides, down the length required. The end is finished off in a similar way to the beginning. It is essential that the string is kept firmly twisted and sewn on securely and straight. See *Basket stitch filling* and *Purl*.

When couching string to pad an interlacing pattern, the string must never be allowed to cross over another piece, but must be cut and butted up to the piece that crosses it. It is then

begun again on the other side of the crossing string, laid so that it again butts up tight against it. These tight butting joins are very important, as otherwise the laid threads may dip as they cross the interlaced section of the design.

PARFILAGE
See *Drizzling*.

PASSING THREAD
See *Threading a needle*.

PASTING THE BACK OF THE WORK.
See *Glue*.

OPPOSITE

235 Melchisadec chasuble, with *or nué*, and pearl embroidery. Made by St Katherine's Embroidery Guild, Southbourne on Sea, *c.* 1925. (*By kind permission of the Dean and Chapter of York Minster*)

PEARL EMBROIDERY

Refers specifically to the freshwater pearls which were found in plentiful supply in the rivers of Russia and Eastern Europe. These were lavishly used to decorate embroideries from these and other European countries. Russia, in particular, had a long tradition, even before the tenth century, of pearl embroidery.

Pearls were also found in the freshwater molluscs of the rivers in Scotland, Yorkshire, Wales, Cornwall and Ireland. The smaller misshapen pearls were collected and sold for embroidery. They were much used for ecclesiastical work during the period of Opus Anglicanum, and in the following centuries they can be seen incorporated into dress embroidery, nearly always combined with metal thread.

PEARL PURL, LAYING

When pearl purl is bought, this coiled wire is springy and unmanageable. But by gently stretching it out, it becomes rigid and easy to manipulate into curves, angles, and any desired line. The coiled wire at the beginning, or where cut, leaves a small hook. This should be turned so that it lies against, or digs into, the background. If the first couching stitching is taken through the first complete coil of the spring, the second stitch can come up behind it to catch the hook firmly down. The third and subsequent couching stitches are taken between

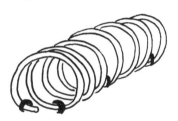

236 Sewing down pearl purl.

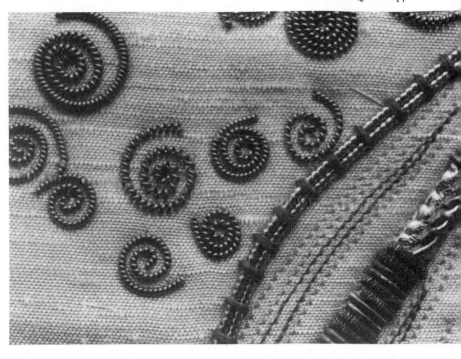

237 Detail of the banner of St John the Baptist's Church, Tisbury. (*Audrey Chorley, the Sarum Group*)

the coils at regular intervals, and should not be seen. The end is finished off in the same way as the beginning. By firmly catching down the wire into the background, it is prevented from catching on anything that might rub it. This can happen very easily, and it may then stretch out of shape and break the stitches holding it. When encircling a shape it is possible to make a perfect join of the wire, so that the join is not seen.

If colour is being used on the embroidery (rather than stitching down the pearl purl with a coloured thread, which gives a rather spotty effect), the following method gives a pleasant result. A cotton perlé is wrapped round the purl pearl so that it falls between the coils. It is then couched down using a matching coloured thread or transparent yarn.

In a laid area it can also add texture with colour. When it is laid against a smooth thread, some of the background colour will glow through the coils. Used as an edging round a motif,

pearl purl is not so heavy as a solid couched thread, and yet often gives just the bite or tidiness to the edge that is required.

Care must be taken when turning an angle not to stretch the pearl purl so that an unsightly length of straight wire is left with no coils!

Pearl purl may also be cut into short lengths and threaded up to be used like beads.

PHRYGIAN GOLD EMBROIDERY

See *Auriphrygium.*

PICOTS

May be worked in passing threads or machine threads, and can add interesting detail. They make a change from looped purl, and may well be a more practical finish on dress or articles that are frequently handled. (*See Fig. 239.*)

PIPING CORD COVERED WITH LEATHER

See *Leather.*

PLAITED BRAID STITCH

See *Elizabethan stitches.*

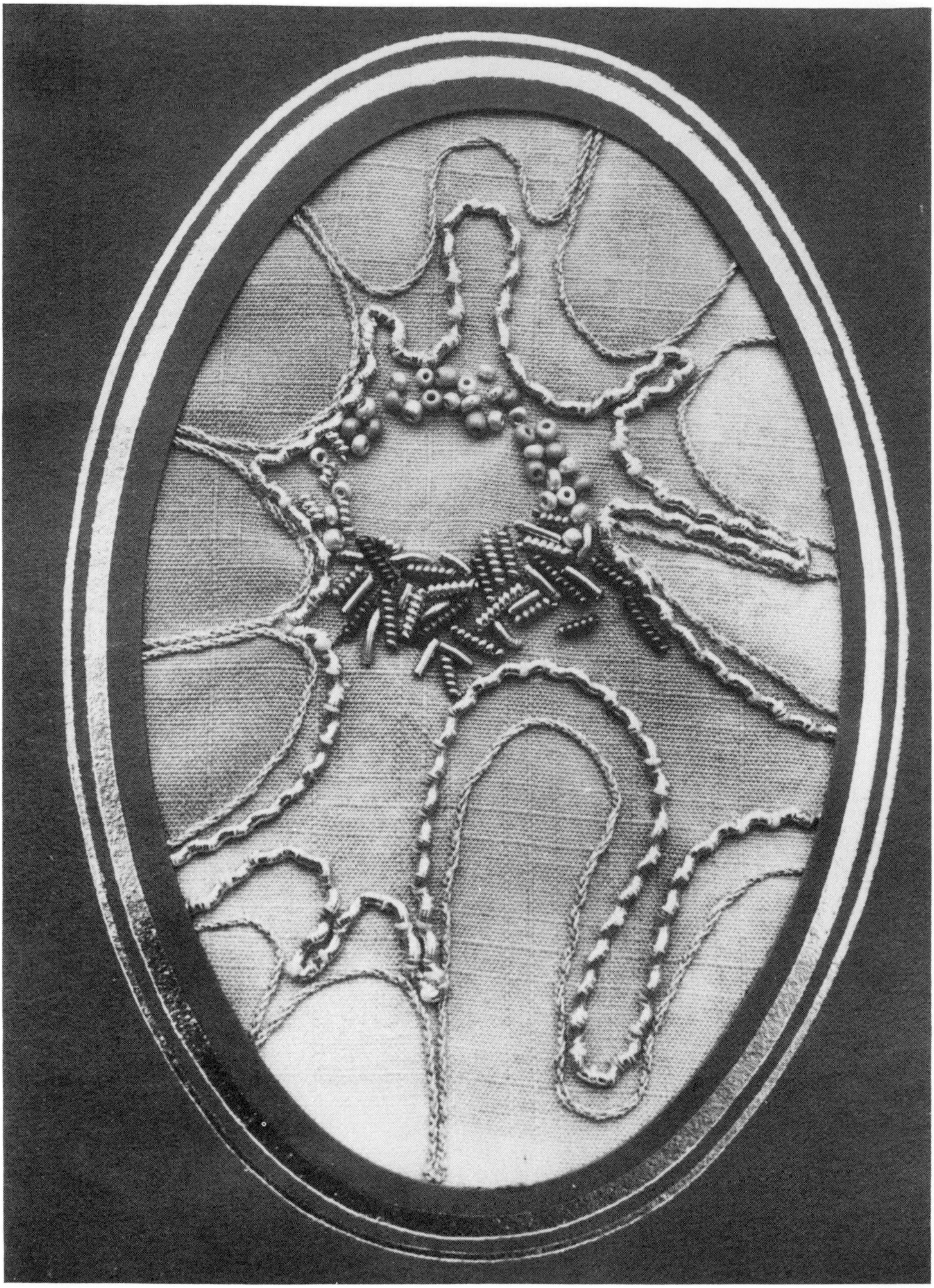

238 Painted fabric with dyed pearl purl. (*Jenny Blackburn*)

239 Picots.

PLAITED STITCH

See *Elizabethan stitches*.

PLATE

The end of the plate is folded underneath itself and stitched down, by taking stitches over it. The plate is then couched down, bending it in a *zig-zag* pattern over the stitches which couch it to the background. The stitches are in this way hidden from view. Plate has a very strong shine, and this zig-zag method of use breaks up the shine, giving an interesting pattern. It can be raised by stitching it in the same way over a piece of string. See *Padding (String)*.

Plate may be crimped by pressing it over a screw to give it a texture. It is then couched in the dents.

When laid flat it is improved if couched with cut purl, which breaks up the hardness, or something of equal interest.

Plate may also be looped or manipulated to combine it with other threads, rolled leather, beads, ribbons and so forth.

240 Panel. Darned scrim background with cordonnet thread. Pulled work techniques with gold threads, picots and purl. 1976. (*Jane Lemon*)

241 Red velvet prayer mat with silver-gilt plate over padding. Indian, probably second half of the nineteenth century. *(Osborne House, Isle of Wight. Reproduced by gracious permission of Her Majesty the Queen)*

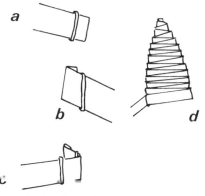

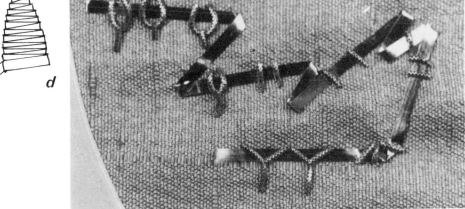

242 Sewing down plate.

RIGHT
243 Plate couched with detached chain and fly stitch in bright check. (*Roma Mason*)

244 Plate worked in a free stem stitch over foundation threads. (*Ann Sutton*)

245 Skirt panel from a 1820 court dress with a floral design worked in solid 'Indian silver' or plate. (*Embroiderers' Guild Collection*)

246 Stole or long scarf. Beaten plate worked diagonally through net. Cairo, first quarter of the twentieth century. (*Embroiderers' Guild Collection*)

PLATERSQUE EMBROIDERY

A style that resembled or copied the craft of the metalworkers. It can be seen in the Spanish ecclesiastical embroidery of the sixteenth and seventeenth centuries

POINT COUCHE RENTRE OU RETIRE

See *Couching (Underside)*.

POWDERING

The term given to the placing of small motifs over a background. During the fifteenth century, beautiful brocades and velvets were imported from Venice, and these were decorated by motifs, worked on linen, applied at intervals over the surface.

PRICK AND POUNCE

See *Transferring a design*.

PUCKERING

All metal thread embroidery, laid work, techniques such as application and manipulation of leather, which require both hands to handle the threads of materials, have to be worked on an embroidery frame. (See *TOOLS: Embroidery frame.*) The tension of the frame is vitally important, and it is essential that it is the same on both the background fabric and the backing calico or linen. The tension must be tight enough to keep the fabrics flat, but if it is drum-tight the fabrics will shrink bank when they are taken off the frame, and unsightly puckers appear. This may not happen until the work has undergone a change in humidity, when the various yarns start to shrink in different manners. Apart from mounting the finished work by stretching it over a hard backing or on a frame, there is little that one can do to alleviate the problem. It may help in some cases to cut out the calico backing.

PULL TECHNIQUE

See *Couching (Underside)*.

PULLED WORK

See *Counted thread*.

PURL

A soft springy coiled wire made in several textures and sizes. It is first cut into the required lengths for threading up and using like a bead. Measure the purl by placing it in position on the work, and cut it using short sharp

247a 'The Poole of London'. (*Lydia Taylor*)

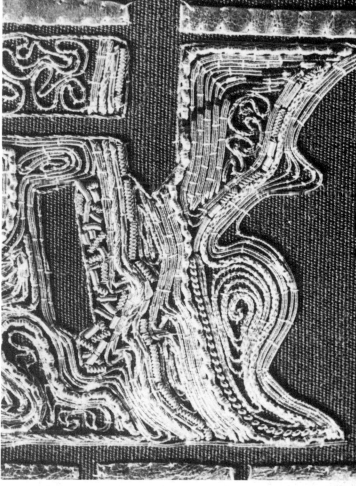

247b Detail.

248 Chessboard filling stitch, but worked with two sizes and textures of purl. The remaining blocks give a few ideas for the many variations that can be worked on a grid with purl.

straight-bladed scissors; then, threading it up, test it in position, as it may well be a fraction too long, or too short. Having established that the length is accurate lay the cut length on a small, felt-covered cutting board. The felt will hold the piece of purl steady. Then, using tweezers to line up the ends, place a length of purl beside the cut piece. Cut off length number two. Continue cutting as many pieces as may be required, always using the first length as the guide. When sewing on the purl, keep back the first cut length as a guide for any further lengths that may be required.

To cut purl to cover a shaped area,

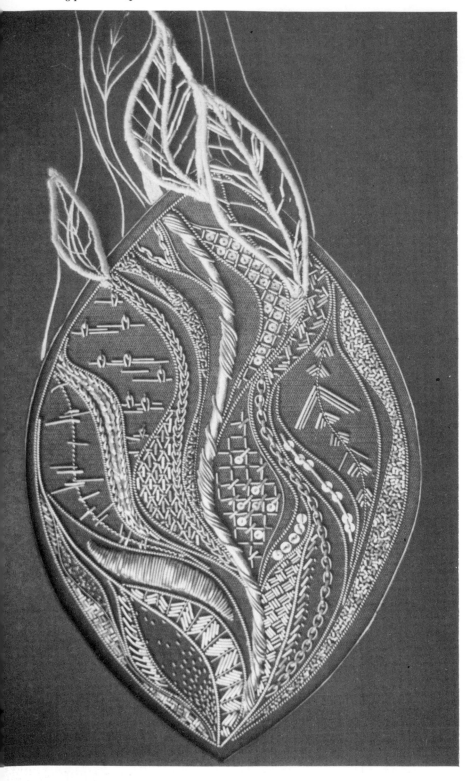

it is easier to cut the longest piece first and then cut each piece progressively smaller. If it is an evenly shaped area, then two pieces of purl may be cut together of an equal length, to be used on the opposite halves of the shape. Test the first two or three pieces cut, to make sure that the angle of decreasing length is correct.

To sew on the purl, use a strong silk, cotton or synthetic sewing thread which has been well waxed. It is as well to take a back stitch after attaching every three or four pieces of purl.

Lengths of purl sewn together in blocks to look like satin stitch give an interesting texture. But the change of direction is important, and needs to be planned at the design stage.

Purl may be sewn over shapes of any of the padding materials or over string, in one texture and size of purl, or mixing them in a planned pattern, or used freely. A decision has to be made as to whether the purl will lie at right angles to the padding, or at a slope; 45° is the usual one used. Purl lying at an angle over string, using mixed textures, can make a very decorative rope pattern.

249 Sampler showing purl in many different patterns and uses. (*Brenda Marchbank*)

250 Purl laid at right angles over string decorated with beaded sequins and beads. (*Audrey Chorley, the Sarum Group*)

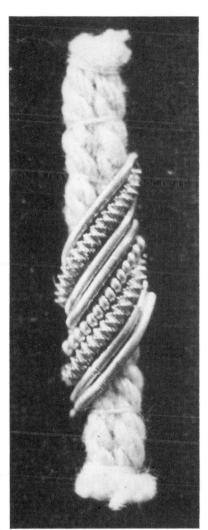

251 Rope pattern. Assorted purls over string. (*Ann Sutton*)

BELOW LEFT
252 Purls laid over string to give rope pattern, mounted on leather over fabric. (*Peggy Hill, the Sarum Group*)

BELOW
253 Late nineteenth-century or early twentieth-century Indian cover with passing thread, purl and purl picots. (*Embroiderers' Guild Collection*)

Purl can be looped, either to lie flat as part of a line or border, or to build up a motif. If it is a long length of purl it may need more control than just the thread running through its centre. A couching thread can be used over the centre of the length, forming a loop, but this is likely to show, either because of the thickness of the thread or because the thread distorts the metal coils. A smaller size of purl, threaded up, can be used as a couch-

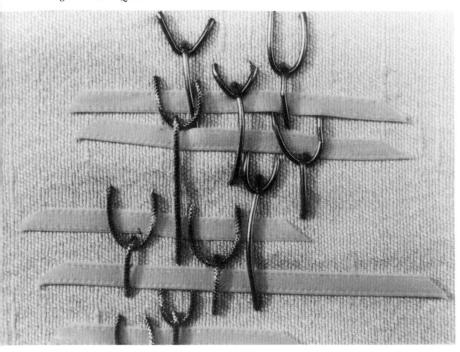

ing stitch. Purl can also be looped so that it stands upright. *Boucles* was an eighteenth-century term for purl loops made by stringing a piece on to a threaded needle which has been taken up through the fabric to the right side. The needle is then returned to the back of the work through the same hole, leaving a loop of purl standing proud on the surface of the work. The loops may be spaced to pattern the ground, or be packed closely against each other to form a textured area. A bead may be attached using a loop of purl (see *Beads*); also sequins, spangles, etc. (See *Sequins*.)

Because purls are springy and soft, they are best used in short lengths. Various embroidery stitches can be constructed from pieces of purl, and they make very decorative blocks, shapes or lines. Stem stitch and chain stitch are only two of the obvious ones.

254 Purls used as fly stitch over ribbon. (*Roma Mason*)

BELOW
255 Smooth purl representing a herringbone stitch to couch ribbon. (*Roma Mason*)

RIGHT
256 Panel, 'Brighton Pier'. Laid threads with assorted uses of purls to give a variation in line and texture. (*Roma Mason*)

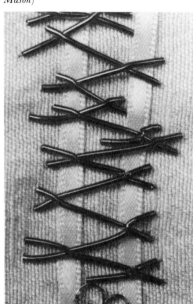

Short lengths of cut purl may be used for couching over threads, twists, plate, strips of leather, for tying down open laid fillings, or for working burden stitch. When cutting purl into the required lengths, a collection of unwanted short, tiny pieces is left on the felt cutting board. This 'grit', as it is called, should be kept safely in a little box, to be sewn on to a flat or padded shape to give a solid texture, or scattered over an area as seeding.

Purl is one of the most versatile metal threads, giving a wide variety of finishes.

QUATREFOILS (Simple)

A form of tracery in architecture, having four arcs separated from each other by cusps (the points where the arcs join). It can also mean 'having four leaves or petals'.

Barbed quatrefoil The quatrefoil is

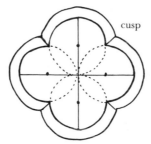

257 Constructing a quatrefoil.

laid over a square; the outline then gives a quatrefoil, with the area where the cusp should be replaced by a right-angled corner of a square.

Interlaced barbed quatrefoil Each arc is interlaced with its neighbouring barbed quatrefoil. This leaves the sections between the main shapes as crosses.

Foliated interlaced barbed quatrefoils These have the additional decoration

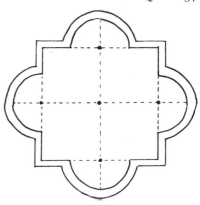

258 Constructing a barbed quatrefoil.

259 Cushion embroidered with coloured silks and metal threads, part of a set of bed furnishings given as a wedding present in 1717. (*By courtesy of the Trustees of the Victoria & Albert Museum*)

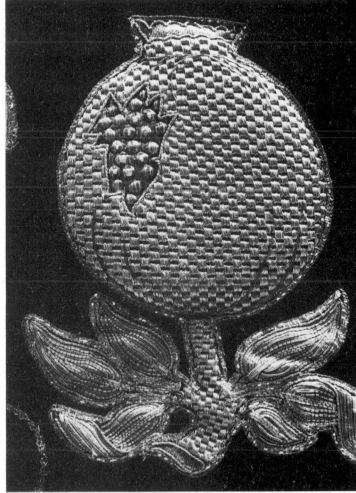

of being formed of boughs or branches of trees.

These types of quatrefoils form the framework of the designs for many of the copes made during the end of the thirteenth century in Opus Anglicanum.

QUILTING

Metal threads have been happily combined with quilting in the past, and with the new metallic threads being so easy to use both in the needle and with the machine, this technique has recently been given some interesting new aspects. Painted and sprayed backgrounds have accentuated the tonal play of light, and metal threads have added a new focus. (*See Fig. 259.*)

RAISED WORK

See *Stumpwork*. Also refers to all highly padded or three-dimensional embroidery. (See *Padding.*) Where raised work has a layered effect, with metal threads on different levels, it is simpler to work each level on a separate frame, than to assemble it at the end, building up to the most padded area.

This leaves only the occasional cord or piece of pearl purl, which is needed to disguise the assembled joins, to be couched through all the layers of padding. See *Motif*. (*See Fig. 261a & b.*)

RANK BADGES

In Imperial China the rank badge was required to be worn by every one of the thousands of civil and military officials appointed by the Manchu emperor, and was worn not only by the man himself, but also by his wife. It was stitched to the centre front of a plain, dark-coloured surcoat (hence the opening down the centre of many examples). A matching badge was attached to the centre of the back. Towards the end of the nineteenth century these rank badges were increasingly mass produced. At this

period one could buy the bird or animal which denoted the degree of rank separately and apply it to the space in the centre of the landscape. This saved renewal of the whole badge when any promotion took place. (*See Figs 45 & 328.*)

RAVEL

Term used for removing woven threads to leave the warp or weft as a fringe. The use of ravelled threads (loose or frayed yarns) in designs has become an important technique, giving movement, change of line and added texture.

RENTRE ET RETIRE

See *Couching (Underside)*.

262 Purse for the Great Seal of England. Silver and silver-gilt on velvet, raised and padded work. English, 1682–5. (*Burrell Collection, Glasgow Art Gallery & Museum*)

263 Torque of couched jap gold with raised ornamented leather discs set in purl, pearl purl or plate settings. (*Mary Johnstone*)

ROCOCO

The ornate decoration of the late Renaissance, which originated in France and predominated in most European countries between about 1710 and 1770. It was characterized by the shell motif and scrolling asymmetrical ornament. The gilded woodwork was reflected in the metal thread embroidery used alongside rich silk stitchery.

264 'Julia's Onions'. The onions are raised and padded with layers of felt and cotton wool, then covered with various shades of gold kid and lamé. Over this layers of silk chiffon and net are highlighted with different weights of pure gold thread. (*Jean Wells*)

265 Frayed gold fabrics, beads and purls. (*Ann Sutton*)

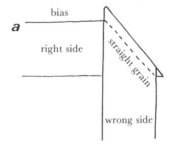

266a To join lengths of fabric cut on the bias. **b** Preparing to turn the rouleau through.

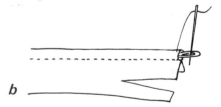

ROMANESQUE

A term covering the early medieval architectural style of the Anglo-Saxon and Norman period which preceded the Gothic. It was at its height in the eleventh century. This style can be seen in the embroidery of the period.

ROULEAUX

May be used to couch down; for weaving through loops and threads; for braiding and plaiting; and to form fringes, tassels, handles and fastenings. But unless they are firm and well made, rouleaux can spoil a piece of work. Strips of material are cut on the bias (See *Bias cut*) from 3 cm (1¼ in.) in width. Any joins must be made on the straight grain. Fold the strip lengthways, right sides togther, and machine the distance required from the edge of the fold. The folded strip should be stretched as much as possible whilst it is being stitched on the machine. Trim off any surplus fabric. The turning should equal twice the width of the machined strip, unless the fabric is very thin and frays easily; in which case a wider turning is left. To pull the roueleau through, insert a bluntended tapestry needle into the open end of the fold, and secure it there by sewing with a fine needle and strong thread through the eye of the tapestry needle and over the end of the opening. Then push the tapestry needle forwards through the fold, and the material sewn to its eye will follow it down the fold. Continue working it through the tube until the rouleau is reversed. If a flat rouleau is required, the turning is trimmed to equal the width of the machined strip. Having pulled it through it should be pressed, making sure that the seam lies on the edge. A round rouleau is not pressed.

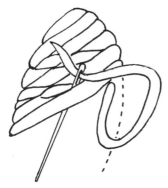

267 Roumanian couching.

ROMANIAN COUCHING

The couching thread is taken across the area, then couched by itself on the return journey. The couching stitch is taken at an angle over the laid thread, more obliquely than Bokhara couching, where the couching stitches are intended to show, and are arranged to form decorative diagonal lines across the area, but not so obliquely as in Oriental couching, where the couching stitch is not discernible.

ROUNDEL

The round part of a design, or a circular motif which is applied to the ground fabric.

RUSSIA BRAID

Best sewn on with a half-back stitch through the centre, as stitching from the side into the centre with the weave leaves a noticeable mark. (For diagram see *Braid*.)

SEEDING (Speckling, Shading)

The application of small stitches to vary the tone in an area by the density of the manner in which they are spaced.

Seeding stitch is formed by a tiny back stitch covered by another one so that it is raised. *French knots* can give the same effect, but stronger. They may be increased or reduced in size by the number of times that the thread is wound round the needle. Other knotted or individual stitches may be used for the same purpose. Chips of purl or grit may be used for seeding. See *French knots*.

Seeding adds texture more than tone when it is self-coloured, like chips of purl on the same-toned background.

SEME

A small regular isolated pattern embroidered over an area of fabric. In heraldry it means 'powdered', whereas in embroidery powdered usually refers to slightly larger isolated motifs or slips.

SEQUINS (Paillettes, Spangles)

Should be attached using a waxed thread. They can be sewn on in several ways. (*a*) With a half-backstitch. Bring the thread up through the background and through the central hole of the sequin. Take a backstitch to the right, to the edge of the sequin, and come up to the far left of the sequin ready to sew on the next sequin, wherever it is required. Half-backstitch can be used to sew the sequins on singly, or in rows where they lie edge to edge. (*b*) With a backstitch. Bring the thread up

268 Velvet hood of Treasurer's Cope, one of a set of five, showing a symbol from the Prisoners of Conscience east window, Salisbury Cathedral. Seeded with french knots. (*Designed by Jane Lemon, worked by Adrianne Woodfine, the Sarum Group. By kind permission of the Dean & Chapter of Salisbury Cathedral*)

through the background and through the central hole of the sequin. Take a backstitch to the right, to the edge of the sequin, and come up on the left hand edge of the sequin ready to take a second backstitch into the central hole. This ties down the sequin with two stitches, one on either side of the central hole. This method can be used to sew the sequins on singly, or in rows where they lie edge to edge. (*c*) The sequins can be attached so that they overlap in a row. The stitching is invisible in this method, as the second sequin covers the stitch on the first. Bring the thread up through the background, over the edge of the sequin, down into the hole and through the background. The needle comes up again, in a back stitch, half a width of

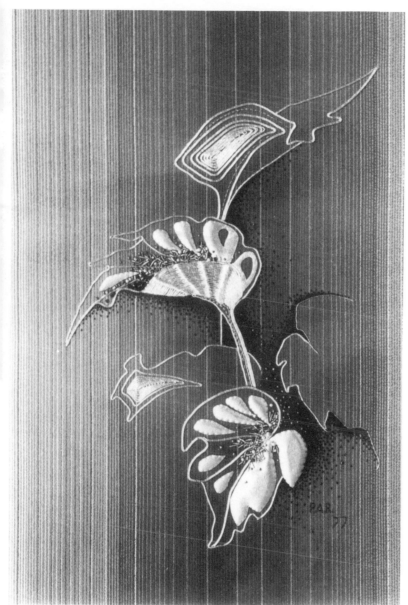

the sequin from where the thread first emerged, ready to attach the next one. (*d*) In some pieces of embroidery the overlapping sequins have been sewn on with two stitches, so that there is a definite line. This forms part of the design, and can give a flow, to the feathers of a bird, for example. (*e*) To fill an area with sequins placed like fish scales, attach one row using a half-backstitch. The second row will lie in between the sequins of the first row, with the central holes in line with the edge of the laid sequins. Continue to attach in this manner. (*f*) Sequins may be attached singly, in rows or to form patterns by sewing on with a small bead. The thread is brought up through the background, through the hole of the sequin and through the bead. The thread then returns through the sequin and background, to be tightened into place. (*g*) The same method is used to tie on the sequin with a loop of cut purl (a boucle), or a small piece of purl, which will lie flat like a bead.

SHAPE – TO LAY THREADS TO FILL

See *Couching*.

269 'Begonia'. Laid gold over string, leather, assorted purls and beads; seeding, mostly french knots. 1977. (Pamela Rooke)

270a Sequin sewn on with a half-backstitch. **b** Single sequin sewn on with a backstitch.

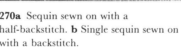

271a Sewing on overlapping sequins invisibly. **b** Sewing on sequins in a fish-scale pattern.

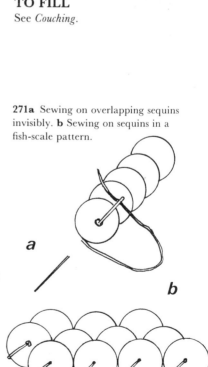

272 Late eighteenth-century cloth of silver veil with solid laid sequins over padding, cut purl and silk on breast area of pelican. (*The Trustees, All Saints' Chapel, Wardour Castle, Tisbury, Wiltshire*)

273 Varied sequins with beads and purl chips, to give a textured area. (*Audrey Chorley, the Sarum Group*)

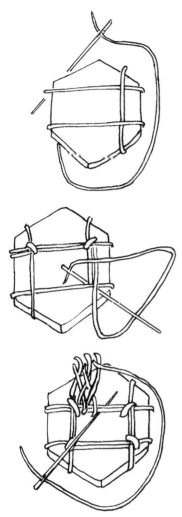

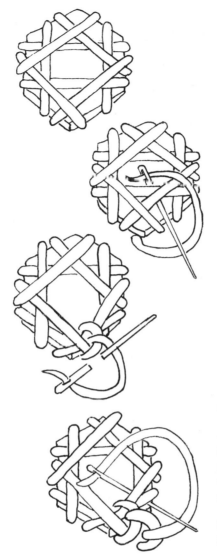

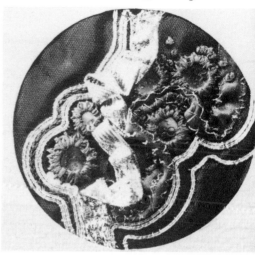

276 Shisha glass incorporated into a modern sampler. (*Ann Sutton*)

274 Sewing on shisha glass with the first foundation and cretan stitch.

275 Sewing on shisha glass with the second foundation and buttonhole stitch.

SHISHA GLASS (Mica)

Shisha glass has no holes drilled in it, so it has to be attached by means of a stitched mount, of which there are several traditional types. (*a*) Four stitches are laid over the glass to make a square. The thread then makes a buttonhole stitch round the crossing of the nearest two threads to hold them together. Forming a double thread round the square, a buttonhole stitch is made at each corner. This forms a firm foundation for working the decorative mount. Cretan stitch may be worked into the background and

round the prepared square of threads. This is a very flexible method, as the cretan stitch can form any shape required with its outside edge into the background. A buttonhole filling stitch may be worked over the same foundation. A buttonhole stitch is made round the threads of the square, the second buttonhole is taken through the background, the third is taken round the threads of the square, and the fourth through the second buttonhole and the background. (*b*) A different foundation may be formed by the first four stitches making a

square as before, then the next four making a second one set at an angle to the first. Thus a right-angled diamond set on a square is the result.

The buttonhole-stitched edge is the usual one used for this foundation, as it has more tension to pull the angled foundation threads into a circle and thus form an attractive setting for the shisha.

SLING
See *Couching (To finish)*.

SMOCKING
Like other techniques, smocking is now being used in new and inventive ways. Not only is it being worked in metal passing and machine threads, but the 'tubes' are being tied together with cut purl and other decorations. As long as the practical use to which the completed piece will be put is taken into consideration, it is exciting to see how these two traditional techniques may work together.

SOUTACHE
See *Russia braid*.

SPIDER'S WEBS
See *Catherine wheels*.

OPPOSITE
277 Silk waistcoat stitched with metal thread and smocked with beads. (*Sue Rangeley. By kind permission of* Embroidery *magazine*)

ABOVE
278 Lurex thread, smocked organza bowl, stiffened by painting with resin. (*Vivien Prideaux, Urchfont Manor City & Guilds Course*)

STAMPED VELVET WORK

The embellishing of the pattern on embossed or stamped velvet. This was usually done with a pair of couched gold threads, or with silk stitchery, taken round the outline of the pattern. A late nineteenth-century technique.

STONES, SEWING ON

Where a stone has a hole through the middle, parallel to the flat back, or two holes, one at either side, it should first be sewn on to the background, using a strong waxed thread, before a decorative mount is worked. On transparent fabric each gem must be sewn on separately, so that the thread is not seen to be carried across the back of the work.

Gold thread may be couched round the gem to form a mount, and if suitable, may be used for sewing the gem to the background. Thread must not be allowed to lie between the stone and the fabric, however, as the stone will wobble, and wear the threads which attach it.

Pearl purl makes an attractive sur-round to a stone. A short length of cut purl can be sewn into the hole, to cover the threads which attach the stone. Alternatively, lengths of purl can be placed to build up a decorative setting to show off the gem.

Beads can be set round a stone, but they should be small enough not to

279 Sprayed, manipulated and smocked panel with smocked frame. (*Michele Hewitt, London College of Fashion*)

280 Stamped velvet outlined with couched jap gold. (*All Saints' Convent, Oxford*)

281 Sewing on stones.

282 Detail of mitre decorated with metal spangles, purl pearl, and stones, in a formalized pattern, *c.* 1850. (*By kind permission of the Dean & Chapter of Norwich Cathedral*)

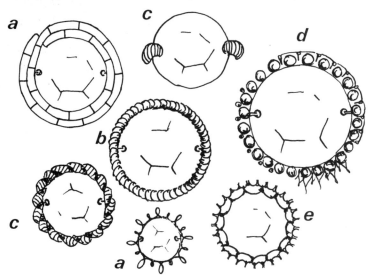

detract from the main point of interest. In each case, the mount must not be too heavy for the jewel.

Where the stone has no hole, it may be attached by a purchased metal mount, if available; or one that has been specially made for it. Otherwise, a mount has to be worked. A fine

passing thread can be used to work a buttonhole or knotted buttonhole stitch through the fabric round the gem. On the second circuit round, the number of stitches is decreased, so that the stitching grips the shape of the stone. If necessary a third circuit may be worked. With some of the strong,

fine metallic threads now available this need not give a heavy result. Alternatively, the stone may be glued on to a piece of felt with one of the modern glues. The felt is then trimmed to leave a narrow edge which can be sewn to the background, then a mount worked as for the stones with holes through them, which should cover the felt surround.

Occasionally, when unusual-shaped stones have been attached, a layer of fine nylon stocking has been laid over them to hold them in position, but this detracts from the effect of the stone. With the very strong modern glues, it should now be possible to stick on the stones. See *Shisha glass.*

STORAGE

Gold work is best kept in an even, dry temperature, wrapped in clean cotton, linen, or acid-free tissue paper, within a calico or linen bag. Plastic coverings are not the best containers, as they can cause condensation if there is a change in humidity. The embroidery should be kept flat where possible, or rolled over a padded roller, with the embroidery on the outside and interleaved with acid-free tissue paper.

283 Picture, 'Esther and Ahasuerus'. Silk and metal thread on satin. Raised and padded work, known as stumpwork, English, c. 1660. (*By courtesy of the Trustees of the Victoria & Albert Museum*)

STRAPWORK

A design used in sixteenth- and seventeenth-century embroidery, which followed the fashions seen in woodwork, plasterwork, and metalwork of the day. It consisted of interlacing bands, and some of the patterns were very intricate. See *Fret*.

STRETCHING (Blocking)

As all gold work is carried out on a frame there is no necessity to stretch it. No metal thread work should ever be stretched, as the method involves dampening the work, which could tarnish and damage the threads, and stain the background fabric.

STRING

See *Padding*.

STUMPWORK (Raised work)

The name given to the English raised work of c. 1640–1688. This three-dimensional work was embroidered over moulds or 'stamps' of parchment, leather, wax and wood, or over padded areas of wool or horsehair, but was probably not referred to by this name until the late nineteenth century. The raised figures, flowers, animals, insects, trees and buildings were covered in close needlepoint stitchery, and trimmed with beads, pearls, spangles, lace and whatever came to hand. Everything was massed together, regardless of scale, to fill every possible space. Metal thread was an important technique in these collectable items, which included caskets, mirrors, book covers, pictures and workboxes.

SURFACE COUCHING

See *Couching*.

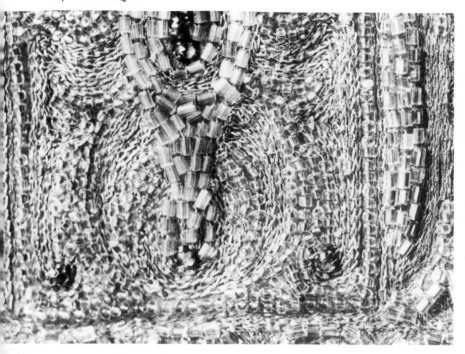

ABOVE LEFT
284 Detail of a panel of a dress. Mauve tambour embroidery in two weights of silver passing thread with beads. French, 1920s. (*Embroiderers' Guild Collection*)

LEFT
285 Ciborium veil, European. Mid eighteenth century, with tasselled edge. (*Embroiderers' Guild Collection*)

ABOVE
286 Tassel on a breaststrap, part of a Moroccan saddle, possibly late eighteenth century. Metal threads are included in the plaiting and used for wrapping. (*Glasgow Art Gallery & Museum*)

SYMMETRY

The exact correspondence of design on either side of a straight line or about a centre or axis.

TACKING

The large temporary stitches holding two or more pieces of material together, whilst the permanent stitches are being worked. A weak cotton thread is used, which easily breaks when removed, so that it does not harm any fibres of the materials. It should always be a pale colour, so that no particles of the dyed thread can colour or mark the work. See *Basting*.

TAMBOUR WORK (Tambour embroidery, Tambouring)

The process whereby a chain stitch is worked with a tambour hook. The fabric, with the design marked on the right side, is stretched tightly in a frame right side up. With the tambour hook in the right hand working on top of the frame, and the thread being fed by the left hand underneath the frame, the hook brings up the thread through the fabric in a loop and works a chain stitch. Motifs can be filled with chain stitch, and rich designs worked in either cotton, linen, silks, wools or a fine pliable metal thread (tambour thread, which retains the name today). The technique may well have originated in China, but it was in India that the use of the ari (tambour hook), gave a style to the embroidery for many centuries; in some areas it is still used today. Tambouring was widely used in England between 1780 and 1850 to decorate the fine muslin and silk dresses of the period, as well as the caps, collars, cuffs, fichus and stoles. It can also be seen to have been used at some stage with most of the various whitework techniques.

Tambour beading The technique whereby the beader holds a string of threaded beads in the left hand underneath the frame holding the tightly stretched fabric. The right hand, using the tambour hook, works on top of the frame with the wrong side of the fabric uppermost. The thread is hooked through to the top of the fabric, between each bead, and looped to make a chain stitch which holds the beads in position. The design is marked on to the wrong side of the fabric so that it can be seen by the worker.

TASSELS

Tassels may be made of any yarn to decorate a garment, accessory or furnishing. Some very ornate ones have been made in the past using metal threads and incorporating purls, spangles, and beads.

A simple tassel may be made by winding the selected yarn round a piece of card, which has been cut to the length of tassel required. Make sure that enough thread is wound round the card to make a generous-looking tassel. Cut the threads along one edge of the card, having prepared a needle threaded with a double length of the same yarn. The needle is

287 Indian invitation case of white silk. The stylized flowers are in padded purl and gold passing. The flaps are finished with a tassel of metal threads. (*Embroiderers' Guild Collection*)

passed through the folded threads, and looped through itself to secure the cut yarn. It is then taken down through the threads so that it can be lost in the tassel. A ball of cotton wool can be placed inside the folded threads to pad up the tassel head to the size required, before tying the threads together with another looped thread. This time the thread is taken up through the top of the tassel, for attaching it when complete. The tassel can now be decorated with detached buttonhole stitch in silk, with purl, as used on regalia, threaded beads, or any other method.

Turk's head knot See *Ball button.*

Ball stitch is an effective way of covering a tassel head. A loop must be formed round the apex of the ball by twisting the threads round each other twice. Do not tighten them at this stage, but keep the left thumb on the knot to keep it from falling apart. A stitch is then taken round the loop, as in fig. 288. This is repeated until the loop is covered, the thread having been tightened. The second and succeeding rows are worked into the previous row of stitches, care being taken that only one stitch comes between each stitch of the row above. As the circumference of the tassel head increases, the stitches become wider to cover the area; *do not* increase them in number, or the forming pattern of diagonal lines will be destroyed. As the circumference decreases again, so the stitches become narrower. When the tassel head is complete, the thread is taken up through the padding to the top, where it is used to attach the tassel.

TENSION

The tension of the sewing thread in metal thread embroidery needs to be even, so that the threads lie firmly without becoming taut or pinched.

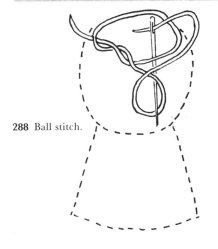

288 Ball stitch.

289 Showing the wooden moulds, one covered in silk, and the completed tassels. (*Hobson & Sons (London) Ltd*)

290 Cut purl, couched circles of twist with chips of purl and beads. (*Audrey Chorley, the Sarum Group*)

This is less easy than it sounds, as one's very mood can affect the way that the needle is pulled through the fabric. Setting up a rhythm is half the battle, but even a good worker needs some minutes to 'warm up' at the beginning of the day. Working at a frame for hours at a time stiffens the back and neck muscles and can cause aches and pains, apart from a tightening of the sewing tension. So get up and walk about at regular intervals, and do neck, back and shoulder exercises. Both you and your embroidery will benefit!

TENSION OF FRAME

See *TOOLS*: *Embroidery frame* and *Pucker*.

TEXTURE

Texture is made by using a wide choice of threads in size, type and tone, and by building up different surface patterns, which with the help of padding vary the planes of the work. Metal thread embroidery has the added advantage of a great reflec-

tive quality, and appreciation of this can greatly add to the changing texture. The direction in which the gold is laid, and the juxtaposition of smooth and textured areas, will add variety to the work. If the design is entirely made up of strong, richly textured threads and techniques the eye has nowhere to rest for contrast, and the whole piece looks dull and flat.

THREADING A NEEDLE

Passing thread Passing has a silk, nylon or cotton core which is wrapped by a fine metal. To thread, unravel the gold for about 5 cm (2 in.), and wax the thread to make the metal section more pliable, and add strength to the core. Push the point of the needle through the centre of the core about a centimetre ($\frac{1}{2}$ in.) from the unravelled point, fold the thread and pass the point of the needle through again, just above the unravelled point. Then thread the needle with the core and the loose unravelled gold which has been pulled out straight. Now pass the

needle through the core where the needle point is already placed, helping the thread to pass over the eye. Trim the loose metal to where it passes through the core for the first time. This prevents the thread from pulling out of the needle, and is the method used by Hobson and Sons' professional workroom where they make regimental badges, insignia and regalia.

Nylon transparent thread Transparent thread or other fine threads which slide out of the needle may be threaded up this way. Double the yarn, and thread the loop through the eye of the needle. The needle is then passed through the loop, so that when it is tightened the yarn forms a knot on the eye of the needle.

TINSEL EMBROIDERY

A fashionable imitation of Turkish embroideries in the late nineteenth century. Simple designs were darned, with a few filling stitches, on net and muslins in gold or tinsel thread. Indian embroidery, although not called tinsel embroidery, was heavily decorated either by stitched tinsel or tinsel fringe. The various gifts to royalty in the nineteenth century were

291 Texture created with manipulated purl, machine stitching and tangled gold threads. (*Ann Sutton*)

294 Threads and purls, creating a lively texture. (*Roma Mason*)

292 Sampler, hand worked, showing varying tones and texture. (*Joyce Hill, London College of Fashion*)

293 Sampler, machine worked, showing varying tones and texture. (*Joyce Hill, London College of Fashion*)

295 Threading a needle. **a** Passing thread. **b** A fine thread.

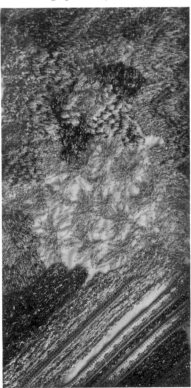

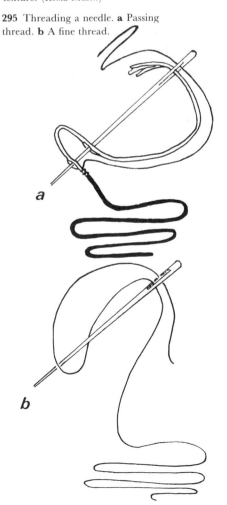

a

b

covered in rich metal thread work and often incorporated tinsel fringe and tassels.

TIR-TIR

Turkish name for gold bullion. See *Byzantine*.

TRANSFERRING A DESIGN

May be done by several methods, depending on the complexity of the design, and the type of fabric used.

Prick and pounce A traditional method, and excellent for detailed designs. The pounce does not hold, however, on a heavily textured fabric, or velvet. (*a*) Place the traced design, right side up, over several layers of felt or a cork mat and prick closely along the design lines with an upright straight movement, using a pricker. (*b*) When completed, rub the back with emery paper (fine sandpaper) to smooth the rough paper round the holes. (*c*) Lay the fabric right side up on a drawing board. Using drawing pins (thumb tacks) or sticky tape, fix it firmly down. (*d*) Lining up the centre line of the pricked design on the centre line of the fabric, fasten the design down on top of the fabric. (*e*) Using a pounce pad (pouncer), dip it into the pounce, and rub it firmly over the surface of the tracing, so that the pounce is forced through the pricked holes on to the fabric. (*f*) When all the pricked lines have been rubbed, carefully lift off the tracing, and gently blow away any superfluous powder that may have collected on the fabric. The dots will rub away at a touch, so the lines must be painted over to fix them. A yellow or white poster paint works well, or thick watercolour. (*g*) When dry, the fabric should be lifted from the board and shaken well to remove any surplus pounce. It is now ready to put on the frame over a backing fabric. See *TOOLS: Pounce, Pounce Pad* and *Pricker*.

For a simple design, the tracing may be pinned on to the fabric, which should already be mounted on the frame, and a medium-sized backstitch is worked through all the design lines.

When completed, the tracing paper is carefully torn or cut away, leaving the tacked lines of the design. If ordinary tacking is used, the stitches will be distorted and/or broken as the tracing paper is removed. It is also difficult to see the design when it is marked only in a broken line, and this very often causes inaccuracies.

Another method for simple designs is to use templates cut from the tracing and backstitched or tacked round to show the design line. Templates may also be chalked round with one of the specially manufactured pencils, or painted round.

Dressmaking transfer paper This may be used for some designs. It is a non-smudge carbon paper and is really only suitable for very smooth surfaces. It must also be remembered that once the design is marked on, the line must be covered, so no second thoughts can take place!

Thin fabrics may be laid over the design, which should be drawn out in black ink, and the design traced through using a pencil.

It is possible to use a perforated tracing prepared for pouncing; first spray the fabric with methylated spirit or benzine, then rub a pounce powder through the pricked holes. Remove the tracing and spray the fabric again. Some art fixative sprays are safe to use on fabric, but it would be wise to test any spray on a scrap of fabric before using it, to make sure that it does not stain. As a safety precaution, use any sprays in the open air.

TRELLIS PATTERN

See *Laidwork*, and fig. 170.

TRELLIS STITCH

See *Elizabethan stitches*.

UNDERSIDE COUCHING

See *Couching (Underside)*.

VELVET TECHNIQUES

Owing to the depth of the pile, many normal embroidery stitches get lost on a velvet ground, so care must be taken as to the methods used. Cords, braids

and heavy threads may be couched into place, composite stitches build up above the pile and work very well, and normal gold work techniques can also be used on velvet if a single layer of thin felt is applied first.

Tudor, Elizabethan and Stuart embroiderers solved the problem by working motifs which were then applied to the velvet, very often with a couched thread or cord to edge it. See also *Opus Anglicanum (Materials)*.

VOIDING

Term used for working the background whilst leaving the design lines or motifs unworked, as in Assisi embroidery.

VERMICELLI

See *Couching (Vermicelli)*.

VOLUTE PATTERN

A spiral or twisting shape.

WARP

The strong, twisted threads which run the length of the fabric. This is called the 'straight grain'.

WATER-SOLUBLE FABRICS

Available for use with either cold or boiling water. The fabric may first be pressed with a warm iron to get rid of the creases. The transparent fabric can be laid over the design and traced through with a pencil; the marks will vanish when the fabric is dissolved. If the boiling water method is being used, you should test that any dyes on the embroidery threads do not run, but nearly all embroidery threads will withstand cold or boiling water.

The machine embroidery may be worked (*i*) in a frame, with the teeth of the machine dropped and the foot removed; or (*ii*) without a frame, using the foot and the teeth raised in the normal position. Make sure that the design is linked by the machine stitching, so that it holds together when the fabric is dissolved. Fine stitching will give a delicate result, while massed stitchery can build up to a heavy lace effect. Because of the variations that can be achieved, the

296 Moroccan saddle. Detail, breaststrap of velvet embroidered with gold. Possibly late eighteenth century. (*Glasgow Art Gallery & Museum*)

297 Plate and jap couched over felt padding with padded purls and an open laid filling stitch. (*Mollie Collins, the Sarum Group*)

298 Formal lace-type motif made with machine stitchery on water-soluble fabric. (*Michèle Hewitt, London College of Fashion*)

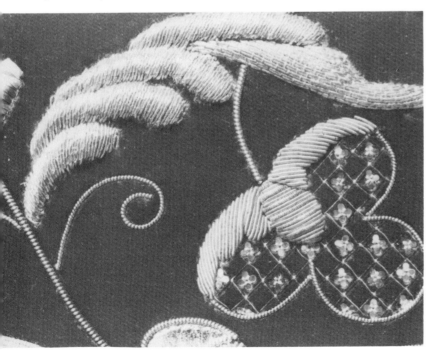

resulting work can make a motif to be applied, or a fabric in its own right.

For soluble fabric made for use with boiling water, the water may be poured over the embroidery, which should be laid in a flat-bottomed dish. After about 15 seconds the water will have cooled, and so the treatment may need to be repeated four or five times until the fabric has dissolved, and the embroidery is soft and pliable. Alternatively, the embroidery may be placed in a saucepan of boiling water and be allowed to simmer. Watch until the material has dissolved – this will be about 30 seconds, depending on the stiffness required for the finished piece.

For soluble fabric made for use with cold water, lay the embroidery in a flat dish and pour cold water over it. Leave as long as necessary. When the fabric has dissolved, pull the embroidery into shape. It will stretch back to its original size, and remain so when dry. It is advisable to lay it on a folded tea towel on a board, and pin out to shape. Do not press it dry with an iron,

as this will flatten the texture of the piece.

WEFT
The threads which weave through the warp threads from selvedge to selvedge on a length of fabric.

WRAPPING
Strips of card, cord, string, rings, and other shapes have all been wrapped with varying threads and yarns to give lively results. These can be applied, couched, woven, plaited, used for fringes and tassels or just used as cords.

Surfaces can be built over string using a zig-zag stitch on the machine. Many items can be wrapped by hand, from frames or mounts for embroidery, to sections of jewellery made from metal thread embroidered motifs.

YEMENITE EMBROIDERY
The Yemenite tradition is one of the oldest. The first Jews emigrated to the Yemen from Palestine in 100 BC and AD 70. This community was cut off

299 Eggs in a nest, using machine stitching on water-soluble fabric. (*Lilian Temple, London College of Fashion*)

OPPOSITE
300 Grid of wrapped card. (*Jenny Blackburn*)

from the mainstream of Judaism for centuries, although there were some outside influences on them over the years. It is thought that many of their practices are very ancient indeed, which is probably also true of their distinctive embroidery. Like the Jewish embroidery of the Mediterranean countries, Yemenite work is used for clothing rather than for ceremonial purposes. In recent years the Israelis have showed them how to adapt their traditional embroideries to more commercial items so that they can market them. See *Jewish embroidery*.

301 'Bravo'. Detail of oil rig panel. Gold jap substitute wrapped and frayed for flare-off. (*Ruth A. Morrison*)

302 Tallit bag with Yemenite embroidery of a traditional design, made for the modern commercial market, *c.* 1970. (*Photograph: Harold Rose*)

PLACES WHERE METAL THREAD EMBROIDERY MAY BE SEEN

Embroiders visiting a museum to see special items or to do serious research, should contact the textile curator well in advance, as very often exhibits are changed, under repair, or not available for study without an appointment. Some collections are not normally open to the public, but it may be possible to make arrangements to visit.

This section is listed by country, except for Britain, which is divided under the headings of counties, with London having its own section. An additional section is devoted to outstanding collections, cathedrals, museums, and other places of interest to embroiderers. Listings have also been given for a few specialist themes and subjects that students may be interested in researching, e.g. Animals, Architecture, Birds, Figures, Heraldry, and Opus Anglicanum. This list is by no means comprehensive, but may provide a starting point.

Directory of places to see metal thread embroidery

ENGLAND

Avon

Bath, Museum of Costume, Assembly Rooms

Bath, Costume and Fashion Research Centre

Bristol, Museum and Art Gallery at Blaise Castle House Items of eighteenth-century dress.

Bristol, St Nicholas Church Museum Small collection of vestments.

Bedfordshire

Luton, Museum and Art Gallery Two pairs of ladies' gloves, seventeenth and late eighteenth century. Child's cuffs (three items only), seventeenth century.

Berkshire

Wargrave, St Mary's Church Work by Sheila Berry. See *Collections*: *Windsor Castle*.

Buckinghamshire

Aylesbury, Buckinghamshire County Museum Number of seventeenth- and eighteenth-century costumes.

Waddesdon Manor Bed valance, French, mid-sixteenth century. Five panels of saints worked in silk, in split stitch, against a ground of couched gold thread. Thought to be French, around 1400.

Cambridgeshire

Cambridge, Fitzwilliam Museum Fragment of fifteenth-century ecclesiastical piece. Man's cap, late seventeenth century. Purse, seventeenth century. Stumpwork panel, English, 1700.

Cambridge University Library Book-covers.

Cumbria

Kendal, Abbot Hall Art Gallery Chinese articles and a few articles of dress.

Derbyshire

Chesterfield, Hardwick Hall Dozen or so panels and domestic pieces.

Derby, Derby Cathedral

Derby, Royal Infirmary Chapel Festal vestments.

Devonshire

Chudleigh, Ugbrooke House English coverlet, 1720.

Exeter, Royal Albert Memorial Museum A few evening bags 1880–1930. Eighteenth-century men's waistcoats, twentieth-century military uniforms.

Dorset

Bridport, St Mary's Church Vestments by Katerin Privett.

C. Durham

Barnard Castle, Bowes Museum Large collection including European ecclesiastical work, fifteenth to eighteenth centuries. Rare items of domestic embroidery, sixteenth and seventeenth centuries. Dress, including fine French eighteenth-century waistcoats. Non-European embroidery and a good Indian section.

Durham Cathedral St Cuthbert's stole and maniple, early tenth century. Cope made for the visit of Charles I, 1633.

University of Durham, Gulbenkian Museum of Oriental Art

Essex

Chingford, St Peter and St Paul's Work by Joyce Williams, 1960–1970s.

See also *Collections*: *Chelmsford Cathedral*.

Gloucestershire

Cheltenham, Art Gallery and Museum and *Pittville Pump Room Museum* Nineteenth-century dress and other examples of ecclesiastical, heraldic and Indian embroidery.

Gloucester, Cathedral

Snowshill Costume Collection To be rehoused in a National Trust property. (Information may be obtained from the Historic Buildings Representative, Severn Regional Office, 34–36 Church Street, Tewkesbury, Gloucestershire GL20 5SN.)

See also *Collections*: *Cathedral of the Forest, Newland*; *Chipping Campden*.

Hampshire

Lymington, St Thomas's Cope with orphreys and hood decorated with lettering by Jane Lemon, 1982.

303 Group of French gaming purses, velvet embroidered with metal thread, incorporating coats-of-arms on bases. (*Founders Collection, the Bowes Museum, Barnard Castle, Co. Durham*)

Winchester, Cathedral Five festival copes, crimson/scarlet/orange velvet and gold lurex with braids and cords, designed by Nancy Kimmins and Moyra McNeill.

Herefordshire

Hereford, Cathedral Several late Victorian and Edwardian pieces.

Hereford, City Museum and Art Gallery

Leominster, Burton Court, Eardisland Chinese and ecclesiastical work, plus 20 or more evening dresses, 1880–1935.

Hertfordshire

St Albans, Cathedral

Ware, St Edmund's College

Humberside

Scunthorpe, Normanby Hall Three uniforms, waistcoat, 1793. 1920–1928 dress and two stoles, plate on net.

Kent

Sevenoaks, Knole House Embroideries in gold appliqué and silver spangles, in the spangle room.

See also *Collections: Canterbury Cathedral.*

Lancashire

Blackburn, Cathedral Vestments.

Burnley See *Collections: Gawthorpe Hall.*

Lancaster, Museum

Manchester, Gallery of English Costume, Platt Hall Costume items of the late

sixteenth, seventeenth and eighteenth centuries. English and European fifteenth- to eighteenth-century vestments, ceremonial bags and purses. Near and Far Eastern robes, strips, etc. Eighteenth to twentieth centuries.

Manchester, Whitworth Art Gallery Many examples, including English sixteenth- and seventeenth-century work, ecclesiastical items and a collection of Turkish towels.

Merseyside, Lady Lever Art Gallery Large collection of seventeenth-century articles and accessories.

Whalley, Nr Blackburn, Stoneyhurst College Fifteenth- and sixteenth-century vestments.

Leicestershire

Leicester, Newarke Houses Museum Two seventeenth-century stomachers, nine

eighteenth-century items of costume, seventeenth-century christening blanket, and two panels, one of which is petit point in silver, late eighteenth century.

Lincolnshire

Lincoln, Cathedral Mary Magdalene altar frontal, Constance Howard MBE, 1964–5.

Lincoln, Usher Gallery One gauntlet, *c.* 1600, with coat-of-arms. Stumpwork workbox, seventeenth-century gloves and several other items of interest.

London

British Museum

Brompton Oratory Vestments.

Church of St James the Less, Pimlico Altar frontal designed by G. E. Street (1824–1881), worked 1861.

Fenton House, Hampstead Four pieces of stumpwork.

Jewish Museum

National Army Museum

North-west Reform Synagogue Work by Kathryn Salomon.

Royal School of Church Music, Addington Palace, Croydon Ecclesiastical work designed by Elizabeth Elvin and Sylvia Green.

Royal School of Needlework

St John's Church, Harrow

St Paul's Cathedral Vestments, Silver Jubilee cope.

Westminster Abbey Vestments.

Westminster Cathedral Vestments.

Westminster Hospital Chapel Altar frontal.

304 St Gregory's Pall. Detail of dolphin motifs in coloured silks, gold, and silver thread on linen applied to black worsted. Early sixteenth century. (*Norfolk Museums Service: Strangers' Hall Museum, Norwich*)

William Morris Gallery One piece only: cushion cover.

See also *Collections: Embroiderers' Guild; Victoria & Albert Museum.*

Norfolk

Kings Lynn, St Margaret's Church Altar frontals by Beryl Dean MBE.

Kings Lynn, Museum of Social History A few items of English nineteenth-century dress and furnishings. Japanese embroidered panels, some richly embroidered gifts presented to royalty on their travels, and one or two other foreign items.

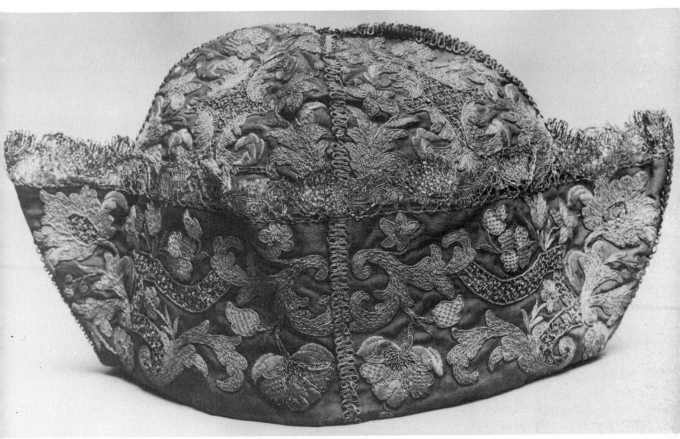

Norwich, Cathedral

Norwich, St Peter Hungate Church Museum Cope that was converted into an altar frontal: silk embroidery with couched gold on linen applied to velvet. English, 1480. Pall from St Gregory's Church, Norwich, 1517, newly restored.

Norwich, Strangers' Hall

Nr Norwich, Blickling Hall About a dozen items.

Oxburgh Hall, Oxburgh Chinese bedspread.

Nottinghamshire

Nottingham, Museum of Costume & Textiles

305 Woman's Reigelhaube or headdress from Bavaria or Salzkammergut. Second half of the nineteenth century. (*Museum of Costume and Textiles, Nottingham*)

Oxfordshire

Oxford, All Saints Convent, Leopold Street A collection of embroidery.

Oxford, Ashmolean Museum, Western Art Department Opus Anglicanum.

Oxford, Bodleian Library Book covers.

Oxford, St John's College Altar frontal made from a cope.

Surrey

Chertsey, Museum Man's embroidered cap, *c.* 1600, pair of gloves, *c.* 1700. Two stomachers *c.* 1730–50 plus other items of eighteenth- and nineteenth-century dress.

Guildford, Museum About six items of dress from the seventeenth and eighteenth centuries. One piece of Opus Anglicanum, 1450–1500. About 15 various pieces of foreign embroidery.

Seale, St Laurence's Church

See also *Collections: Embroiderers' Guild; Guildford Cathedral.*

306 Gentleman's cap, early eighteenth century. (*Castle Howard, Costume Galleries, York*)

Sussex

Parham Park A number of pictures, a state saddle and sixteenth-century satin embroideries for the Great Bed.

Worthing, Museum Four pieces only including two pairs of men's gloves, mid seventeenth century.

Warwickshire

Sutton Coldfield, Oscott College Fifteenth- and sixteenth-century vestments.

See also *Collections: Coventry Cathedral.*

Wiltshire

Tisbury, Church of St John the Baptist Work of Audrey Chorley, 1970s.

Wardour Castle Chapel

Salisbury, Cathedral Te Deum frontal,

c. 1900. Annunciation frontal, *c.* 1900. Work of the Sarum Group from 1978.

St Thomas' Church Piece of Opus Anglicanum, Lady Chapel altar frontal by Pat White (the Sarum Group).

Salisbury and South Wilts Museum Stumpwork mirror frame, gauntlet gloves of Charles II.

Worcestershire

Worcester Cathedral, the Library Fragments of a stole and maniple found in the tomb of Bishop William de Blois, twelfth century.

Yorkshire

Halifax, Bankfield Museum Fifteenth-century ecclesiastical work, Chinese raised work.

York, Minster Historic pieces. Work by the York Minster Broderers, 1970s–1980s.

Castle Howard, Costume Galleries Wide collection of uniforms, church vestments and domestic items. Seventeenth century onwards.

SCOTLAND

Aberdeen, Anthropological Museum, University of Aberdeen Twenty or so items collected in the Balkans, mostly modern Albania, in the 1920s.

Aberdeen, Art Gallery and Museum A few Oriental items which include metal thread with the silk. Some twentieth-century evening dresses.

Edinburgh, Royal Scottish Museum Italian mitre, late seventeenth century, articles of costume.

Glasgow, Burrell Collection

Glasgow, Gorbals Parish Church Work of Hannah Frew Paterson.

Glasgow, Museum and Art Gallery Only a few items, in the Ethnography department.

Hamilton, the Old Parish Church Pulpit fall by Hannah Frew Paterson, mid 1980s.

See also Edinburgh, Glasgow.

AUSTRIA

Lower Austria, Monastery of Zwetti

Salzburg, St Peter's Abbey

Upper Austria, Monastery of Kremsmunster

Vienna, Convent of the Visitation

Vienna, Kunsthistorisches Museum Imperial mantle made in Sicily for the coronation robe of the Holy Roman Emperor, 1133. Made in the Imperial Workshops at Palermo. Gold on red velvet, depicting a tiger fighting a camel.

Vienna, Weltliche und Geistliche Schatzkammer Vestments of the order of the Golden Fleece, second half of the fifteenth century. These are a large set of vestments decorated with technically excellent *or nué* embroidery.

BELGIUM

Antwerp, Rockoxhuis Cabinet mounted with small panels of coloured silks and metal thread embroideries.

Brabant, Averbode Abbey Remarkable series of vestments, sixteenth century.

Brussels, Musees Royaux d'art et d'histoire Rupertsberg altar frontal, 1200–1230. Gold and silver threads with silk in stem and satin stitch.

Ghent, Church of St Michael

Maaseik, St Catherine's Church Chasuble of St Harlindis and St Relindis, and the veil of St Harlindis, remodelled in the middle ages. Gold and silk on linen. The veil has blue and green glass beads, pearls and copper-alloy bosses. Ninth century, believed to be the earliest known english work.

CZECHOSLOVAKIA

Brno, Moravska Galerie Orphrey of a chasuble, Bohemia, 1350–1400. The Crucifixion, with a laid gold ground, silk split stitch figures with some *or nué.*

Cleb Musée Municipal

Prague, National Museum Textile collection of Jewish embroidery.

FRANCE

Chartres, Cathedral Treasury Mantle for the statue of Our Lady of the Pillar. French seventeenth-century raised work and couching in gold and silver thread.

Evreux, Musée Municipal Mitre of Archbishop Jean de Marigny, first half of the fourteenth century.

Haute Savoie, parish church Mitre, second half of the fourteenth century.

Lyon, Musée Historique des Tissus Many pieces.

Metz, Cathedral Treasury Cope of Charlemagne, Byzantine, late twelfth century.

Paris, Cluny Museum Altar hanging of the first half of the fifteenth century. Opus Coloniense yellow background picked out in silver; architectural canopies frame episodes from the lives of St John and St Mark. Orphreys and mitres. Chasuble, gold on red velvet depicting the leopards or lions of England. This is believed to have been made in England at the beginning of the fourteenth century as a horse trapper, and remade in the eighteenth century.

Paris, Musée de Louvre Buckler, Charles IX of France. Casket, first quarter of the seventeenth century.

Paris, Musée des Arts Decoratifs Chasuble 1735.

Paris, Musée de Versailles

Paris, Russian Cathedral Vestments.

Saumur, Château Pieces of orphreys, crosses, vestments, sixteenth-century black velvet, Spanish, with laid gold, *or nué* and cords. Cope, late sixteenth century, red velvet and brocade. Chasuble, green.

Sens Cathedral, south-east of Paris Vestments of St Edmund Rich. Stole and maniple of St Thomas à Becket. Fourteenth-century *aumonière* (alms purse).

St Bertrand de Comminges, Cathedral Opus Anglicanum cope with laid gold background; 34 birds and 66 beasts are contained by the linking compartments. Early fourteenth century.

307a Pulpit fall for the Old Parish Church of Hamilton, 50 × 135 cm (20 × 53 in.). The gold leather three-dimensional cross which is the focal point of the design is echoed by a red silk cross spanning a background mosaic of symbols. Many different symbols are incorporated in the pattern, including the bee, lily-of-the-valley, ram's head, spider's web, butterfly, anchor and dolphin. Many three-dimensional methods were used in the making of the details, combined with traditional gold work techniques. (*Hannah Frew Paterson*)

307b Detail of 307a

308 Cope of red velvet with orphreys and hood embroidered in gold and silk threads. The velvet has motifs showing the Ascension of the Virgin, angels, double eagles with fleur-de-lys, and bells. The hood shows the Virgin enthroned, and the orphreys have saints and apostles: Zita, Bartholomew, Catherine, Jesaja and Philip. On the canopies over the heads of the saints is an English coat-of-arms (portcullis). English, first quarter of the sixteenth century. (*Rijksmuseum, Amsterdam*)

Troyes, Cathedral Treasury Purse, fourteenth century. Gold threads couched on canvas, with appliqué and raised work.

Var, Church of St Maximin Cope, late thirteenth century.

GERMANY

Bamberg, Cathedral Treasury

Hamburg, Museum Für Kunst und Gerwerbe

Munich, Bayerisches National Museum Chasuble, metal threads and coloured silks on red satin. Three panels of strapwork in couched gold, with basketwork floral shapes, cover the vestment. The coats-of-arms of Casmir Anselm of Mainz, Elector between 1629 and 1647, dates the piece. Altar frontal from Bamberg Cathedral, couched gold and silk on linen, *c.* 1300.

GREECE

Athens, Benaki Museum Icon of St George, Constantinople, 1729. This high-quality piece was worked by the nun Agatha in silks and metal threads on a red silk background, with a horse in silver. Epitaphios, a Byzantine embroidery by Despoineta, 1682.

Museum of Greek Popular Art

HOLLAND

Amsterdam, Rijksmuseum A small amount of fifteenth- and early sixteenth-century ecclesiastical work.

HUNGARY

Budapest, Hungarian National Museum

INDIA

Ahmedabad, Calico Museum of Textiles

ISRAEL

Jerusalem, Israel Museum

ITALY

Anagni, Cathedral Treasury Altar frontal, Rome or central Italy *c.* 1300.

Ascoli Piceno, Palazzo Comminale Cope, 1275. The design depicts episodes in the lives of 16 Popes.

Assisi, San Francesco Treasury Dossal, probably made in Sicily, early thir-

teenth century. Yellow silk twill worked in couched gold thread. The interest lies in the design, which incorporates pairs of birds, dogs and mythical creatures.

Cortona, Treasury of San Francesco Superfrontal and set of vestments made for Cardinal Silvio Passerini between 1517 and 1526, and presented to the Cathedral of Cortona. The vestments were designed by painter Andrea Garbo, 1466–1527. The work is in *or nué* of superb quality.

Florence, Museo di S. Maria del Fiore Or nué panels depicting the life of John the Baptist, designed by Antonio del Pollainolo. They were incorporated into a set of vestments, but were remounted individually in 1730.

Florence, Museo Nazionale de Bargello First floor chapel, important altar frontal of the period Florence 1336.

Florence, Pitti Palace, Museo Degli Argenti Vestments with laid gold orphreys 1499–1500.

Perugia, Cathedral Museum Or nué orphreys on a cope. Mitre, seventeenth-century gold work set of vestments. Many chasubles of all periods.

Rome, Vatican Museum and Treasury Cope of St Sylvester, Opus Anglicanum, early fourteenth century and one of the finest examples. Good collection of vestments.

Sienna, Cathedral Museum Splendid vestments and frontals of various periods with some fine metal thread embroidery.

Trento, Cathedral Treasury

Venice, S. Maria Della Salute Chasuble, Venetian, between 1929 and 1949. Green silk with gold embroidered orphreys: pelican and lamb with other symbols, birds and animals.

POLAND

Wawel, Cathedral Treasury

ROMANIA

Bucharest, Museum of Art

RUSSIA

Azerbaijan, History Museum

Leningrad, State Russian Museum

Leningrad, Hermitage Museum

Moscow, Historical Museum

Ryazan, Regional Museum

Zagorsk, Historical Art Museum

SPAIN

Barcelona, Case de la Disputacion, Capilla de San Jorge Altar frontal, St George and the Dragon, Catalonia *c.* 1460.

Museum of the History of the City

Museum of the Sacred Vestments of the Monastery of Guadalope

Textile Museum

SWEDEN

Skara Cathedral Chasuble, French, 1275. Salmon pink silk with metal threads in underside couching.

Stockholm, Nordic Museum

Uppsala, Cathedral Treasury Cope, French, 1274.

SWITZERLAND

Basel, Historisches Museum

Berne, Bernisches Historisches Museum Altar frontal, Austrian, 1340–50, from the convent of Konigsfelden. Fine groupings and portraiture with strong architectural details, laid gold background.

Fribourg, Gruyere Castle

UNITED STATES OF AMERICA

Baltimore, Walter's Art Gallery

Boston, Museum of Fine Arts

Brooklyn, Museum

Chicago, Art Institute of Chicago

Los Angeles, County Museum of Art

New York, Cooper-Hewitt Museum of Decorative Arts & Design

New York, Smithsonian Institute

New York, Jewish Museum

New York, Metropolitan Museum of Art Early fourteenth-century chasuble, Opus Anglicanum silk and metal thread on red velvet.

Ohio, Cleveland Museum of Art

Washington, D.C., Hillwood Russian ecclesiastical textiles.

Collections and places of special interest

BURRELL COLLECTION, GLASGOW

Ecclesiastical vestments of the fourteenth, fifteenth and sixteenth centuries; articles of costume and home furnishing.

CANTERBURY CATHEDRAL, KENT

Five copes designed by Beryl Dean, MBE. Vestments. Jupon of the Black Prince.

CATHEDRAL OF THE FOREST, ALL SAINTS CHURCH, NEWLAND, GLOUCESTERSHIRE

Low Mass set in cream. black and gold, and a pulpit fall designed by Beryl Dean, MBE.

CHELMSFORD CATHEDRAL, ESSEX

Set of white vestments, altar frontal and hangings in machine embroidery and appliqué, by Barbara Dawson. Altar frontal by Beryl Dean and Pat Scrase. Banner – Virgin and Child, with a border of angels' wings.

CHIPPING CAMPDEN, GLOUCESTERSHIRE CHURCH

Altar frontal, fifteenth century. Cope.

COSTUME AND FASHION RESEARCH CENTRE, BATH

COVENTRY CATHEDRAL, WARWICKSHIRE

Lady Banner commissioned for the Mothers' Union. By Margaret Nicholson, 1970.

EMBROIDERERS' GUILD

(Apartment 41, Hampton Court Palace, East Molesey, Surrey KT8 9AU)

Members may come to the headquarters at Hampton Court Palace, where the Guild houses a world-famous collection of historical embroidery, a library and bookshop. There are classes and workshops on all aspects of contemporary embroidery and study sessions on historical embroidery, when examples from the Collection may be handled. For home study or teaching, members may borrow folios containing samples of embroidery, photographs, slides, notes and suggested reading lists. These fo-

309 Pair of gloves, leather with silk and silver-gilt thread on silk satin. English, 1600–1650. (*Burrell Collection, Glasgow Art Gallery and Museum*)

lios cover all embroidery techniques. Books may also be borrowed from the extensive library. There are regular exhibitions, a programme of social events, and outings to places famous for their embroideries. Members also receive a newsletter twice a year. Membership of the Guild, an educational charity founded in 1906, is open to anyone interested in embroidery. The headquarters are open only to members, not to the general public.

Affiliated branches

There are over 100 branches of the Embroiderers' Guild throughout the United Kingdom, which arrange their own programme of events, and subscription rates. Branch members receive the newsletter and may borrow books and folios through their Branch Secretary, but have to pay extra to attend events at headquarters such as workshops, exhibitions and outings.

Young Embroiderers' Society

Aims to help and encourage those under 18 who would like to embroider. A newsletter is published three times annually, with ideas for using fabric and thread in interesting and creative ways. Workshops and classes are arranged and resource packs on different aspects of embroidery are available.

Embroidery Magazine

The Guild's quarterly magazine publishes imaginative and authoritative articles on contemporary and historical embroidery in addition to reviews, saleroom reports, and a diary of exhibitions, workshops and courses. *Embroidery* is available by subscription from the Guild, or may be ordered through newsagents.

GAWTHORPE HALL, BURNLEY, LANCASHIRE

Textile collection of the Hon. Rachel Kay-Shuttleworth.

310 Ciborium veil, European (South Germany?). Mid eighteenth century. White satin embroidered with silver-gilt thread, plate, purl and spangles, with some coloured floss silks. Laid and couched work with long-and-short stitch. (*Embroiderers' Guild Collection*)

GUILDFORD CATHEDRAL
Cope by Beryl Dean MBE.

ROYAL SCHOOL OF NEEDLEWORK
(Hampton Court Palace)
The Royal School of Needlework was founded in 1872 by HRH Princess Christian, daughter of Queen Victoria, with the object of restoring ornamental needlework to the high place it once held amongst the decorative arts. Over the years, much outstanding embroidery has been undertaken by the School's workroom, including the coronation robes worn by Queen Elizabeth, now the Queen Mother, in 1937, and Queen Elizabeth II in 1953. The workroom undertakes commissions, repairs and cleans lace and samplers. It also conserves and restores antique embroideries and tapestries, stretches canvases, and makes banners to order. Under the apprenticeship scheme, pupils are taught all forms of highly specialized needlework techniques. The Design Room interprets customers' requirements into individual designs, both traditional and modern. The school has day and evening classes, and short courses in all types of embroidery for both skilled embroiderers and amateurs.

TEXTILE CONSERVATION CENTRE
(Apartment 22, Hampton Court Palace).

The Textile Conservation Centre, a registered charity, was set up in April 1975 to fulfil a need for the scholarly conservation of historic textiles. The centre is a teaching and working organization where students attend planned courses in the academic, scientific and practical technique of research and conservation of textiles as historic documents. In 1982, the Friends of the Textile Conservation Centre were formed to support the aims of the Centre. For further details, please write to the Director, Mette Tang Simpson, at the above address.

VICTORIA & ALBERT MUSEUM, LONDON
An extensive textile collection of all periods and from all over the world, with fine examples of metal thread embroidery representing each style.

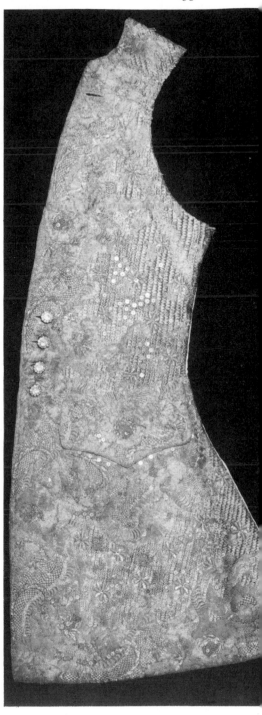

311 Chinese fragment with couched
metal thread. (*by kind permission of the
Trustees of the Rachel Kay-Shuttleworth
Collection, Gawthorpe Hall*)

312a&b Mid eighteenth-century
waistcoat. Woven gold background with
heavy string at intervals on the warp, and
crystal buttons. Free gold embroidery
forms a border from the shoulder down
the front and around the hem. (*By courtesy
of the Trustees of the Victoria & Albert
Museum*)

312b Detail of 312a.

Opus Anglicanum – Syon Cope, 1300–1320, Steeple Aston Cope, now cut into a dossal and frontal. Butler Bowden Cope.

Altar frontal with the portrait of Ralph Nevill, fourth Earl of Westmorland with his seven sons on one side, and on the other Lady Catherine Stafford and her thirteen daughters. They were married in 1523.

Pall or hearse cloth belonging to the Worshipful Company of Saddlers.

English, early sixteenth century. Portrait of three ladies worked in silks, metal threads with spangles.

English man's waistcoat in a wide variety of metal threads and techniques on a woven gold background, mid-eighteenth century.

English embroidered dress, c. 1740, which is a magnificent example of the work of this period.

Excellent examples of Byzantine embroidery, Jewish embroidery for all

purposes, Chinese robes, badges etc. are also among the items found in this fine collection.

WINDSOR CASTLE, BERKSHIRE

St George's Chapel, the Rutland Chantry Group of panels based on New Testament themes in mixed techniques and metal thread embroidery. Beryl Dean MBE, 1970.

Themes and subjects

ANIMALS

Cluny Museum, Paris Horse trapper.

Embroiderers' Guild

Kunsthistorisches Museum, Vienna Coronation robe of the Holy Roman Emperor, 1133, Palermo – tiger attacking a camel.

San Francesco Treasury, Assisi Thirteenth-century dossal.

St Bertrand-de-Comminges Cathedral, France Opus Anglicanum cope with 66 beasts in the linking compartments of the design. Early fourteenth century.

Victoria & Albert Museum, London Opus Anglicanum copes, Erpingham chasuble (fourteenth century).

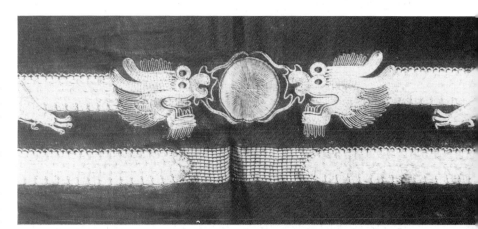

ABOVE RIGHT

313 Cuff, dragons in couched gold thread. Chinese. (*By kind permission of the Trustees of the Rachel Kay-Shuttleworth Collection, Gawthorpe Hall*)

RIGHT

314 Lion, detail of Ting Kia; Chinese armour of fabric with plates secured on the inside by round-headed rivets, giving the outer surface a rich appearance. Worn by military officials of the Emperor's court in the middle of the nineteenth century. See also Fig. 11. (*Glasgow Art Gallery and Museum*)

315 Letter case, or kincob, presented to Queen Victoria 1887 or 1897. Animals and hunter worked in purl, with sequins, pearls, and pearl purl. Indian. (*Osborne House, Isle of Wight. Reproduced by gracious permission of Her Majesty the Queen*)

316 Velvet-covered tube which contained an address of congratulations to Queen Victoria on the occasion of one of her Jubilees, 1887/1897. A sacred bullock and flowers in assorted purls. (*Osborne House, Isle of Wight. Reproduced by gracious permission of Her Majesty the Queen*)

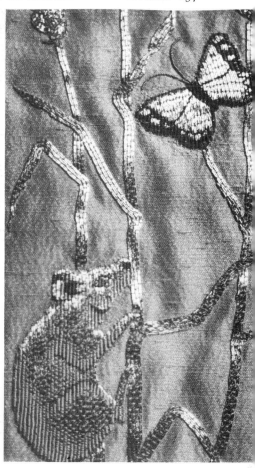

318 Gold dupion stole end, one of three stoles worked by newly trained gold workers, 1983. (*York Broderers. By kind permission of the Dean & Chapter of York Minster*)

317 Benedicite chasuble, green brocade; back orphrey, with spider, grasshopper and squirrel on formalized leaves in gold work, heavily padded. Made by St Katherine's Embroidery Guild, Southbourne-on-Sea, *c.* 1925. (*By kind permission of the Dean & Chapter of York Minster*)

319 Fabulous beast. (*Sheila Miller*)

320 Hood of a cope. Silver and silver-gilt thread and coloured silks in split stitch and couched work on linen. Italian, late fifteenth century. The central figure of silk, linen and gilt thread tissue, German (Cologne), late fifteenth century, replaces the original embroidered figure, most of which has disappeared. (*By courtesy of the Trustees of the Victoria & Albert Museum*)

ARCHITECTURE

Berne, Bernishes Historisches Museum Austrian altar frontal, 1340–50.

Blackburn Cathedral Set of Low Mass vestments; design is based upon the architectural features of the cathedral. Pamela Waterworth, 1978.

London, Victoria & Albert Museum Opus Anglicanum Copes

Paris, Cluny Museum Altar hanging, first half of the fifteenth century. Opus Coloniese.

Salisbury Cathedral Red and white chasuble sets, 1984. Pat White, Sarum Group. Spire hanging, 1987. Sarum Group.

321 Detail of letter case, or kincob, presented to Queen Victoria on the occasion of one of her Jubilees, containing an address of congratulations. Shows Agra Taj worked in purl. Indian. (*Osborne House, Isle of Wight. Reproduced by gracious permission of Her Majesty the Queen*)

BELOW

322 Festal chasuble, detail of shoulder line. Design taken from the vaulting of the Cathedral. (*Pat White, the Sarum Group. By kind permission of the Dean & Chapter of Salisbury Cathedral*)

OPPOSITE

323 One of ten sections of the 3.5 m (11ft 6in.) 'Spire hanging', showing the west front of Salisbury Cathedral to commemorate the 1985 Spire Appeal for six and a half million pounds. (*Designed by Pat White, worked by Catherine Talbot, the Sarum Group*)

324 Indian runner in white satin, gold bead fringe. Peacock, raised and padded. Coloured silks with laid gold, purl and pearl purl, beads. (*By kind permission of the Dean & Chapter of Canterbury Cathedral*)

325 Whole palm-leaf fan. Silver-gilt plate on satin. Made in Aden; presented to His Majesty George V on his accession to the throne, 1911. (*Osborne House, Isle of Wight. Reproduced by gracious permission of Her Majesty the Queen*)

BIRDS

Canterbury Cathedral   Vestments.

Embroiderers' Guild

Metz Cathedral Treasury   The cope of Charlemagne, Byzantine, late twelfth century.

Salisbury Cathedral   Baptistry, hanging with the Dove. Audrey Chorley, Sarum Group. 1980.

St Bertrand de Comminges Cathedral Opus Anglicanum cope with 34 birds in the linking compartments of the design. Early fourteenth century.

Assisi, Italy, San Francesco Treasure Yellow twill dossal, Sicilian, early thirteenth century.

York Minster Altar frontal and vestments.

326 Eagle, late nineteenth or early twentieth century. Japanese. (*All Saints' Convent, Oxford*)

OPPOSITE

327 Stole, part of replica of vestments of St Thomas à Becket, made in east Kent, 1890. (*By kind permission of the Dean & Chapter of Canterbury Cathedral*)

ABOVE

328 Chinese rank badge in couched metal threads. Note that the bird has been worked and applied as a separate motif. (*By kind permission of the Trustees of the Rachel Kay-Shuttleworth Collection, Gawthorpe Hall*)

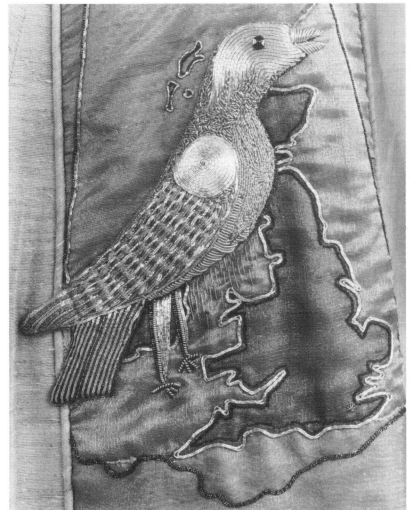

329 A detail from the orphrey on the Addington Palace cope, adapted from the coat-of-arms. The cope was worked as a co-operative scheme in memory of Dorothy Wigg, who attended there. (*Devised by Elizabeth Dakers, designed by Sheila Berry, directed by Elizabeth Elvin. The Royal School of Church Music, Addington Palace*)

330 Veil from festal set, with two doves worked in metal threads for St Mary's Church, Wargrave. (*Sheila Berry*)

331 Birds. Organza moon, metallic threads and assorted techniques. (*Diana Saunders*)

FIGURES

Coventry Cathedral Lady Banner by Margaret Nicholson.

Durham Cathedral Stole and maniple.

Embroiderers' Guild

Italy, Florence Or nué panels.

Victoria & Albert Museum, London Opus Anglicanum, stumpwork, work from all periods.

Windsor Castle, St George's Chapel Panels by Beryl Dean, MBE

The majority of the ecclesiastical embroidery in the thirteenth, fourteenth and fifteenth centuries depicts figures.

332 Osprey. (*Connie Pepper*)

333 Cope, the Tree of Jesse. Red silk embroidered with silver-gilt, silver thread and silk in underside couching and split stitch, with laid and couched work. English, 1295–1315. (*By Courtesy of the Trustees of the Victoria & Albert Museum*)

OPPOSITE

334a Hildesheim Cope. Laid silver-gilt and coloured silk threads in brick stitch. German, late thirteenth or early fourteenth century. (*By courtesy of the Trustees of the Victoria & Albert Museum*)

335 Band embroidered with figures of saints. Inscribed in Armenian, probably eighteenth century. (*By courtesy of the Trustees of the Victoria & Albert Museum*)

OPPOSITE BELOW

334b Detail of 334a.

336 Virgin in quatrefoil on hood of cope. Laid gold and mixed techniques on red velvet. Second half of twentieth century, embroiderer unknown. (*By kind permission of the Archbishop of Canterbury*)

337 Panel for a triptych. A seraphim worked in *or nué*. Jap gold couched with filoselle. (*Beryl Dean, 1958. Embroiderers' Guild Collection*)

338 Motif on altar frontal, mid 1920s, made by Watts & Co. (*By kind permission of the Dean & Chapter of York Minster*)

339 Festal high altar burse. Late nineteenth century. (*By kind permission of the Dean & Chapter of Canterbury Cathedral*)

340 'Syd'. Face embroidered with russia braid and jap. Variety of threads and purls used for the hair. (*Brenda Marchbank*)

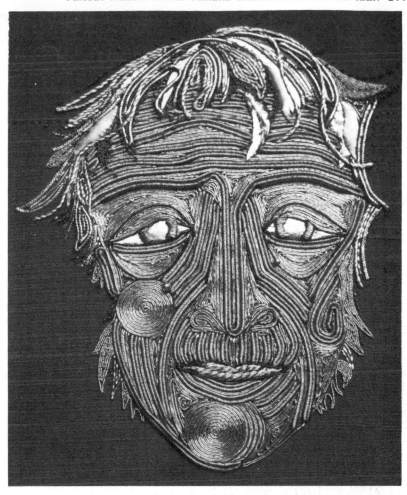

341 Two Peruvian stick dolls (detail). Couched cords and braids, 1975. (*Constance Howard* MBE)

342 'Icon'. Metallic knitting yarn halo. Imitation jap, sequin waste, gauze, purls and beads. (*Ruth Duckitt*)

343 'Lady with cornucopia'. 10 × 8 cm (4 × 3 in.) (*Margaret Hall*)

344 The Syon Cope was originally a bell-shaped chasuble and belonged to a complete set of mass vestments, of which some of the other vestments, embroidered with coats-of-arms, have been used to make the orphreys and the morse. St Simon is shown in this cut-off barbed quatrefoil. (*By courtesy of the Trustees of the Victoria & Albert Museum*)

HERALDRY

Burrell Collection, Glasgow Bag for the Great Seal of England.

Salisbury Cathedral

Victoria & Albert Museum, London Fourteenth-century stole and maniple, Syon Cope. Altar frontal with the portrait of Ralph Nevill, fourth Earl of Westmorland, and his seven sons on one side, and on the other that of Lady Catherine Stafford and her thirteen daughters. They were married in 1523.

LETTERING

Bodleian Library, Oxford Book covers.

Durham Cathedral St Cuthbert's stole and maniple.

Embroiderers' Guild Various articles.

Radley College, Abingdon Altar frontal by the Sarum Group, 1985.

St Thomas' Church, Lymington Cope with lettering on orphreys and hood by Jane Lemon, 1982.

Salisbury Cathedral Hangings and altar frontal in the Baptistry and Chantry. Sarum Group, 1980.

Victoria & Albert Museum, London

York Minster

OPPOSITE

345 Banner of the Worshipful Company of Broderers, 1564. Detail of lion supporter. (*By kind permission of the Master, Wardens and Court of Assistance of the Worshipful Company of Broderers*)

346 Banner of the Worshipful Company of Broderers. The coat-of-arms itself consists of paly of six argent and azure, on a fesse gules between three lions of England passant guardant or, two broches saltirewise between as many trundles or (quills of gold thread). Late sixteenth century. (*By kind permission of the Master, Wardens and Court of Assistance of the Worshipful Company of Broderers*)

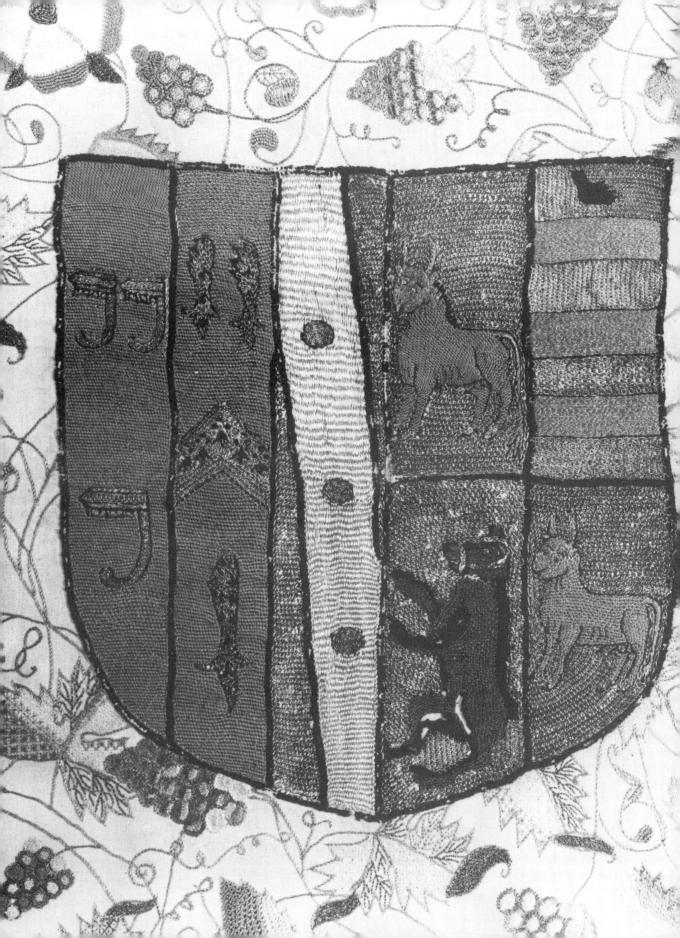

347 Embroidered pillow cover showing detail of the coat-of-arms. English, 1592. (*By courtesy of the Trustees of the Victoria & Albert Museum*)

348 Sachet, linen embroidered with silver thread and silks in tent stitch. English late sixteenth century. (*By courtesy of the Trustees of the Victoria & Albert Museum*)

349 Letter case, or kincob, enclosing an address of congratulations to Queen Victoria on the occasion of one of her Jubilees. Lion and unicorn worked in purls on velvet. Indian. (*Osborne House, Isle of Wight. Reproduced by Gracious Permission of Her Majesty the Queen*)

OPUS ANGLICANUM

Anagni, Italy

Ascoli Piceno, Italy

Ashmolean Museum, Oxford

Bologna, Italy

Guildford Museum, Surrey

Madrid, Spain

Metropolitan Museum, New York

Pienza, Italy

St Bertrand de Comminges, France

St Thomas' Church, Salisbury

Toledo, Spain

Vatican Museum and Treasury, Rome

Vich – Nr. Barcelona, Spain

Victoria & Albert Museum, London

350 The West Yorkshire Regiment, the Prince of Wales's Own Badge, to be applied on to a chairback in the Sanctuary of the Regimental Chapel, York Minster, as a refurbishment after the 1984 fire. (*Lt. Col. J. R. C. Allen*)

OPPOSITE ABOVE
351 Part of City and Guilds heraldry research sheet. (*Michèle Hewitt, London College of Fashion*)

OPPOSITE
352 Marnhull orphrey, detail. English embroidery, *c.* 1300. (*By courtesy of the Trustees of the Victoria & Albert Museum*)

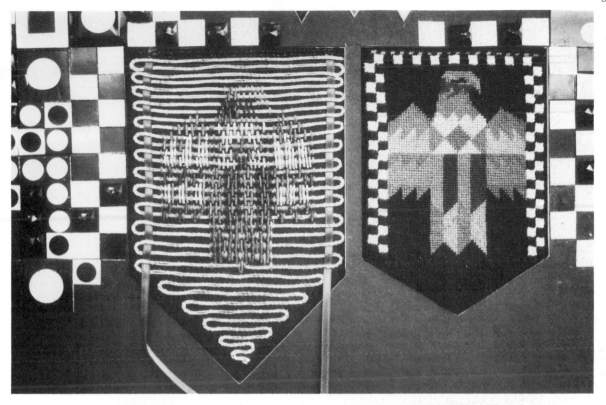

Cope	Date	Background
Jesse	1295–1315	Red twill weave
Salzburg	Late thirteenth to early fourteenth century	
Ascoli Piceno	Late thirteenth century	Silver-gilt thread
Anagni	Late thirteenth century	Silver-gilt thread
Madrid	Mid thirteenth to early fourteenth century	Silver-gilt thread
Syon	1300–1320	Silver-gilt, silver and silk thread underside couching
Vatican	1300–1320	Red twill silk
Steeple Ashton	1300–1320	Beige twill silk ground, metal thread background
St Bertrand de Comminges	1300–1320	Silver-gilt thread
Butler Bowden	*c.* 1330–1350	Red velvet
Vich, Spain	*c.* 1325	Velvet
Bologna	Early fourteenth century	Silver-gilt thread
Toledo	Early fourteenth century	Silver-gilt thread
Pienza	Early fourteenth century	Silver-gilt thread
St Sylvester's (Vatican Museum)	Fourteenth century	Silver-gilt thread
Salzburg		Silver-gilt thread
Chasuble Vienna	1300	Purple twill silk, silver-gilt, silver and silk threads
John of Thanet Panel: Christ enthroned (Victoria & Albert)	100 × 42 cm (39½ × 16½ in.). 1300 (panel)	Blue twill silk

Framework	Subjects in linking compartments and main subject
Scrolling design from Tree of Life	'I am the true vine' – ancestors in each scroll
Scrolling tree spreading from Tree of Life	
Geometric arrangement, circles	
Geometric, circles	
Barbed quatrefoils	Angel playing upon a viol
Barbed interlaced quatrefoils	Six winged seraphim, heraldry for orphrey. St Michael and the apostles, life of Christ and the Virgin
Barbed quatrefoils	
Foliated barbed quatrefoils	Heraldic lions. Scenes from life of Christ and Virgin
Circles of foliated design	Thirty-four birds, sixty-six beasts. Foliated human mask, lion mask
Foliated arcading	Winged angels, lion masks, acorns with pearls. Coronation, Adoration, Annunciation
Foliated, arcaded	Winged angels. Lombardic lettering
Arcaded	On the slightly threadbare background an interesting design of scrolling oak branches and geometric devices is exposed in places, but the worker has couched the gold ground in chevron diapering throughout
Arcaded	
Arcaded	Two seraphim stand on wheels holding crowns
Arcaded	Some tent stitch. Original hood, very tiny
Barbed quatrefoils	Successive stages of Crucifixion on each side. Wild rose, vine leaves
Arcaded setting, seated Christ	Powdered with gold lions rampant. Arcaded setting, gold mantle bordered with lions, eagles, and dragons. Richly jewelled

Further reading

BRIDGEMAN, Harriet and DRURY, Elizabeth, *Needlework: An Illustrated History.* Paddington Press, 1978

CHILD, Heather and COLLES, Dorothy, *Christian Symbols.* Bell, 1971

CHRISTIE, A.G.I., *English Medieval Embroidery.* Oxford, 1938

CHRISTIE, Mrs Archibald, *Samplers and Stitches.* Batsford, 1929

CLABBURN, Pamela, *The Needleworker's Dictionary.* Macmillan, 1976

CONNELL, Patrick, *Greek Ornament.* Batsford, 1968

DAWSON, Barbara, *Metal Thread Embroidery.* Batsford, 1976

DEAN, Beryl, *Ecclesiastical Embroidery.* Batsford, 1958

— *Ideas For Church Embroidery.* Batsford, 1968

— *Embroidery In Religion and Ceremonial.* Batsford, 1981

— *Church Embroidery.* Mowbray, 1982

de DILLMONT, Thérèse, *Encyclopaedia of Needlework,* DMC Library from about 1886

de SAINT-AUBIN, Charles Germain, *Art of the Embroiderer.* Kudos and Godine, 1983

GRAY, Jennifer, *Machine Embroidery.* Batsford, 1973

JOHNSON, Beryl, *Advanced Embroidery Techniques.* Batsford, 1983

JOHNSTONE, Pauline, *Byzantine Tradition in Church Embroidery.* Tiranti, 1967

Opus Anglicanum. Exhibition Catalogue, Victoria & Albert Museum, London, 1963

RUSSELL, Pat, *Lettering for Embroidery.* Batsford, 1971, 1985

SNOOK, Barbara, *English Historical Embroidery.* Batsford 1960, Bell & Hyman 1974

SPEISER, Noemi, *The Manual of Braiding,* Noemi Speiser, 1983

SWIFT, Gay, *Batsford Encyclopaedia of Embroidery Techniques.* Batsford, 1984

EMBROIDERERS' GUILD PRACTICAL STUDY GROUP, *Needlework School.* Windward, 1984

THOMAS, Mary, *Mary Thomas's Embroidery Book.* Hodder and Stoughton, 1964

WARDLE, Patricia, *Guide to English Embroidery.* London, HM Stationery Office, 1970

WINDSOR FRY, Gladys, *Embroidery and Needlework.* Pitman, 1953

Also see *Embroidery* magazine published quarterly by the Embroiderers' Guild.

Suppliers of materials

Beads
Creative Beadcraft Ltd
Unit 26
Chiltern Trading Estate
Earl Howe Road
Holmer Green
High Wycombe
Bucks HP15 5QT

The Warehouse
39 Neale Street
Covent Garden
London wc2

Beads, tambour hooks
Ells and Farrier
5 Princes Street
London W1

Calicos of different weights, wide selection of fabrics prepared for dyeing or painting. Water-soluble fabric
Whaleys (Bradford) Ltd
Harris Court Mills
Great Horton
Bradford
West Yorks

Ecclesiastical supplies, cloth of gold and lurex, braids, cords, ribbons
Watts & Co Ltd
7 Tufton Street
Westminster
London SW1

Haberdashery, Bondina by the metre
MacCulloch and Wallis Ltd
25–26 Dering Street
London W1R 0BH

Japanese braiding equipment, pattern books, etc
Roderick Owen

38 Argyle Street
Oxford OX4 1SS

Lamés, lurex nets, paper lurex and the unusual
Barns Yarns
Old Pitts Farm
Langrish
Petersfield
Hants GU32 1RQ

Leather
John P. Milner
Cilycwm
Llandovery
Dyfed SA20 0SS

Silken Strands
33 Linksway
Gatley
Cheadle
Cheshire

Lurex fabrics and wide range of all fabrics
Borovick Fabrics Ltd
16 Berwick Street
Oxford Street
London W1V 4HP

Metal threads and general embroidery supplies
Crown Needlework
23 High Street
Hungerford
Berks

Metal threads and all other embroidery supplies. High quality metal thread, cords, etc. of all types
Mace and Nairn
89 Crane Street
Salisbury
Wilts

Royal School of Needlework
25 Princes Gate
London SW7 1QE

Metallic threads, wide range for hand and machine as well as general embroidery supplies including curved needles
Shades
57 Candlemas Lane
Beaconsfield
Bucks HP9 1AE

Metallic and lurex threads including copper purls
Stephen Simpson (Tinsel Products) Ltd
Avenham Road Works
Preston
Lancs

Silk fabrics including silk tweeds
Hera
87 Heathcroft
London NW11 7HL

P. N. Jones Trading
18 Holly Grove
Peckham
London SE15 5DF

Sussex Silks
Oakenwood House
Cinder Hill
Horsted Keynes
Haywards Heath
West Sussex

Silk threads, thrums
Silken Strands
33 Linksway
Gatley
Cheadle
Cheshire

Threads and fabrics
The Campden Needlecraft Centre
High Street
Chipping Campden
Gloucestershire

SUPPLIERS IN THE USA

Aerolyn Fabrics Incorporated
380 Broadway (Corner of White
Street)
New York

Appleton Brothers of London
West Main Road
Little Compton
Rhode Island 02837

American Thread Corporation
90 Park Avenue
New York NY 10016

Bucky King Embroideries Unlimited
121 South Drive
Pittsburgh
Pa 15238

Craft Yarns
PO Box 35
Pawtucket
Rhode Island 02862

Lily Mills
Shelby
North Carolina 28150

Macey's
Fifth Avenue
New York

The Makings
1916 University Avenue
Berkeley
California 95704

The Needle's Point Studio
7013 Duncraig Court
McLean
Virginia 22101

The Rusty Needle
1479 Glenneyre
Laguna Beach
California 92651

The Sun Shop
7722 Maple Street
New Orleans
La 70118

Tinsel Trading Company
7 West 36th Street
New York 18